INHERITANCE OF HORSES

INHERITANCE
of
HORSES

JAMES KILGO

James Kilgo

The University of Georgia Press
Athens and London

Published by the University of Georgia Press
Athens, Georgia 30602
© 1994 by James Kilgo

Designed by Sandra Strother Hudson
Set in 10.5 on 14 Sabon by Tseng Information Systems, Inc.
Printed and bound by Thomson-Shore, Inc.
The paper in this book meets the guidelines
for permanence and durability of the Committee on
Production Guidelines for Book Longevity
of the Council on Library Resources.

Printed in the United States of America
98 97 96 95 94   C   5 4 3 2 1

Library of Congress Cataloging in Publication Data

Kilgo, James, 1941–
Inheritance of horses / James Kilgo.
p.   cm.
Contents: Indian givers—Mountain spirits—Coming off the
back of Brasstown Bald—High blood—Open house—Taken
by storm—A gift from the bear—According to
Hemingway—Inheritance of horses.
ISBN 0-8203-1640-7 (alk. paper)
1. Georgia—Social life and customs. 2. Outdoor life—
Georgia. 3. Kilgo, James, 1941–   —Homes and haunts—
Georgia.   I. Title.
F291.7.K55   1994
975.8—dc20   93-41176

British Library Cataloging in Publication Data available

For

CAROLINE LAWTON KILGO

and

JOHN SIMPSON KILGO

(1912–1991)

CONTENTS

ACKNOWLEDGMENTS

For their help in reading and preparing parts of the manuscript, the author thanks Bob Benson, Stan Lindberg, Maura Mandyck, Karen Perry, and especially Susan Aiken.

Some of these essays first appeared in the following publications: "Indian Givers" and "A Gift from the Bear" in *Gettysburg Review,* "Mountain Spirits" in *Sewanee Review,* "Coming off the Back of Brasstown Bald" in *Oxford American,* "Open House" in *New England Review/Breadloaf Quarterly,* "Taken by Storm" in *Boats: An Anthology.*

INHERITANCE OF HORSES

OYSTERCATCHERS

BACK WHEN we were young enough to believe that the rest of our lives would take forever, Ocean Isle Beach was undeveloped, an empty stretch of marsh and sand, naked to the south Atlantic sun. Someone had recently built a bridge from the mainland, and if you looked closely you could see where developers had staked out streets and lots, one of which belonged to my father, but on that day in May we had the island to ourselves—two couples still new at the business of adulthood.

We had met Dick and Sandy nine months before, soon after he and I arrived at the University of Georgia, and had quickly discovered common ground. All connections worked. Everybody liked everybody, and we all loved an empty beach. At Ocean Isle that day, we walked the edge of the surf for a mile or more, picking up shells, then returned to the car for a picnic. When we had eaten, Dick and I left our wives stretched out in the sun and went off in search of birds.

He was interested. Birds were a reason to get outdoors, something to do. But I was driven, Adam in the Garden still naming creatures I had never seen before. And this was my first birding trip to the coast in the spring. When the road stopped at the south end of the island, I hopped out of the car and headed toward the marsh.

"Wait a minute," Dick said. "I thought we were going to the beach. I'm barefooted."

"It's low tide," I explained. "The birds are on the mudflats. Come on."

I forged into the tall spartina, into the hot, sexual smell of the salt marsh, towing Dick in my wake by naming the birds we might find on the creek—marbled godwit, whimbrel, dowitcher, maybe even a long-billed curlew—sturdy, northern European names for umber-colored birds.

"This better be good," he said.

The creek and the mudflats I expected had been ruined by developers. They were dredging and filling in the marsh, turning that fragile habitat into solid ground for houses. The banks of the creek were piled high with mud, dried gray in the sun. But look: scattered about on the mounds of mud, a host of birds, all of a kind—blocky black heads and long, bright red bills— dozing one-footed in the glare. Though they were new to me, I recognized them instantly as oystercatchers. Whether they actually ate oysters or not, I didn't know, but I was sure they didn't *catch* them. Maybe they caught them open. I brought one bird into focus: against that black plumage, a startling yellow eye encircled by a scarlet ring. And the red bill, as long as a table knife and almost as thin. It looked just right for slipping through the slightly opened crack of a bivalve. And there were eight of them.

Dick and I eased forward for a closer look, and the oystercatchers flushed. In flight their wings and backs showed a surprising chevron pattern in brown and white, and they cried woefully as they flew—*wheep, wheep, wheep*. Dick agreed that they were worth the ordeal of slogging barefooted through the marsh.

We walked fast on the way back, both of us thinking of the six-pack of beer iced down in Dick's trunk. Halfway across, Dick flinched, stopped, swore, and lifted his foot. The heel was bleeding heavily through the caked black mud. "Damn, Kilgo. Looka here." We had stumbled into a bed of oysters.

Dick stooped and picked a cluster from the mud. Then he picked another. "Grab as many as you can carry," he said. "We'll have a feast."

"What about your foot? It looks pretty deep."

The oysters were not as exciting to me as they were to Dick. I had made valiant attempts at gulping them down raw, most recently at a famous New Orleans oyster bar, but as much as I wanted to like them it just hadn't worked.

"Hurts like hell," he said. "But leaving these oysters ain't going to make it feel any better."

So I picked a muddy double handful, bunched tongues of shell, sharp enough indeed to cut deep.

Dick hobbled along in front, walking on the side of the injured foot, making bloody tracks in the mud.

We reached the car, but Dick continued on, limping through the hot, loose sand of the high dunes, down to the hard wet beach, down to the surf. We dropped our oysters in the shallow waves, and Dick, leaning on my shoulder, swished his foot back and forth in the water. "Son of a bitch," he said. Then he lifted it, clean of sand and mud, and held it up for our inspection. The cut was deep all right and still bleeding, though not as heavily as before.

"That might need stitches, Dick."

He sat down on the sand, peeled off his T-shirt and tore from it a strip with which he bound his wound. Then he stood, grabbed my shoulder for a crutch, and said, "Now let's see about these oysters."

With his free hand he gathered up an armload, and I managed the rest. Back at the car, I opened the trunk and reached for a couple of beers. Dick took out his pocketknife. "You have to be careful," he said.

He chopped at the ridge along the seam—anybody home?— then inserted the blade into the crack near the base of the shell, twisted the knife, and the shell opened with a reluctant little suck. The oyster reposed in water, plump and shiny and gray-ish brown. Dick slid the blade beneath the oyster, cutting the adductor, then offered it to me. To have turned it down would have been unthinkable. I took a swallow of beer first. Then I took the oyster and drank it from the shell—drank brine, blood, the smell of marsh mud, and the sharp, piercing cries of the oystercatchers.

By the time we finished the oysters we were down to one beer apiece. Dick's foot was throbbing. He wanted his wife to doctor it. He handed me the keys. I drove fast, feeling wild and raunchy and salted to the gills. The girls, I thought, might be sunbathing topless.

But they had seen us coming while we were still a long way off, and when we got there, they were gathering up, folding up, putting stuff away. Leaving a tidy site.

Part 1

INDIAN GIVERS

Some time or other, you would say it had rained arrowheads,
for they lie all over the surface of America.
HENRY DAVID THOREAU

MOST of the boys I grew up with were more interested in play-
ing baseball and football than they were in hunting and fishing
and camping, but I was different. Until I was twelve or thirteen, I would rather have found an arrowhead than hit a home
run. I had no more hope of doing one than the other, however,
assuming that most of the arrowheads in our part of the state
had already been collected. Had it not been for the Dargans, in
fact, I would probably have concluded that arrowheads were
as extinct as the ivory-billed woodpeckers, but the boys of that
family proved by continued success that at least a few remained.

The Dargans lived in the country. Among the five children
was a boy of my age named Freddie. Our fathers had been
friends before us, so it seemed to me that Freddie and I were
born already knowing each other. From weekends spent in his
home I learned that finding an arrowhead required a talent, an
eye, as hitting a baseball does. Freddie and his brothers had it
but not I. We were crossing a plowed field one day, not looking
for relics but going fishing. Suddenly, Freddie stopped, stooped
over, and picked up something. He brushed the sand off and
held it out: "Pretty little bird point." I don't know if my hands
actually trembled when I took it—flaked flint, hard and sharp,
an artifact of the wild, aboriginal past—but I was in awe, as

though it had the power to impart a deeper knowledge of the savage life it stood for.

Too quickly Freddie took the arrowhead back and dropped it into his pocket. When we reached the edge of the field, he stooped over and picked up another one. "That's not fair!" I wanted to scream. I kicked at a clod of dirt in consternation, angry, as though I had been intentionally wronged by someone in authority. "Why can't I ever find one?" I whined.

The reason, I concluded, was that I lived in town, whereas the Dargans were country people, had been since Indian times. When I learned in fifth-grade South Carolina history of the traffic between Indians and the early colonists, it was Dargans I pictured, trading with naked warriors at the edge of a deep green forest, the same green forest that stretched away from the back fields of Freddie's place to the Pee Dee River swamp. From one generation to the next, I assumed, Dargan forebears had handed down their memories of the old, wild life. I was powerfully drawn to that. In that same South Carolina history book there was a picture of Indians, living beneath the canopy of a spreading, moss-hung oak. They ate acorns, the text said. Sometimes, especially in the fall, Freddie and I might come upon such a tree in the woods, and I would feel so strongly that the place was hallowed by an Indian presence that I could almost make myself believe I saw them, feathers and paint, slipping away through the dim trees. Back at the house, Freddie and his brothers, sometimes even their father Mr. Hugh, would speak of Indian ways with such authority and familiarity that I came to regard them as the appointed stewards of Indian lore in our part of the state. No wonder they had a drawer full of arrowheads.

It was clearly understood, of course, that the artifacts were theirs and not mine. When I looked covetously upon their riches, they said, "That ain't nothing. You should have seen the collection Daddy had that got burned up. He had ten times this many."

They were referring to a fire that destroyed their parents' house before they were born. How could an arrowhead burn up? I wondered. I had thought that stone would be impervious to fire.

"They just all turned to dust. When you tried to pick one up, Daddy said, it just crumbled in your hand."

As an adult I spent many years as an avid birder, tramping through fields and forests that must have been strewn with arrowheads, but it was not until I became a hunter that I began to find them. The first ones were crude—the clumsy white quartz points that occur in the Piedmont of Georgia. But as I became more skillful, hunting deer and turkeys along the lower Savannah River in South Carolina, I finally found a good one, the kind of arrowhead I had been longing for since childhood.

I was hunting deer that day with a man named Jay, an amateur archaeologist who had enough Cherokee blood in his veins to claim some right to what he was doing and enough knowledge to do it right. The plantation where we were hunting is two hundred miles downstream from the old Cherokee territory, but it is an area rich in artifacts. Twenty years earlier, a Harvard graduate student named Stoltman had investigated several sites on the property. Though I had not read his monograph, I understood that he found evidence of ancient and intensive occupation.

On that gray and windy afternoon, Jay noticed a spot on the edge of the swamp that looked promising to his practiced eye and decided that he would rather hunt relics than deer. When I asked what he saw in that particular twenty acres, he mumbled something about elevation and proximity to the river swamp. But those features were not unique to the field he had in mind. "It feels right" was all I could get by way of further explanation.

And of course he turned out to be right. Almost immediately we began finding shards of pottery and pieces of worked flint. "This is a site," Jay proclaimed.

Two hours later we were still looking, down a firebreak plowed along the edge of the swamp. "Just like the other times I've actually gone out looking for arrowheads," I thought. "Be intentional about it and you don't find the first one." My expectation of spying something so small and so specific in an area so vast dimmed with the closing day. Finally, I started back to the truck alone. An arrowhead, I was thinking, must be the kind of thing you have to catch out of the corner of your eye, like a certain kind of starlight or the shimmer of sun on the flank of a deer; a focused gaze won't see it. And there it was, caught, sure enough, out of the corner of my eye—displayed on a pedestal of sand, as though the earth itself were handing it to me, clean and reddish orange, as triangular as the head of a rattlesnake and sharp enough to pierce a heart.

The poet Coleman Barks has written of the moment a child discovers under the Christmas tree the shiny red tricycle he has longed for but not dared to expect. What does the child do? He ignores it, intent on every trivial and accessory present he can find until at last there is nothing left to open. When the lustrous arrowhead caught my eye, I picked it up, dropped it into my pocket, and kept on walking.

But I played with it in my pocket all the way back to the truck, testing its thinness between my thumb and forefinger, the keenness of its edges against the balls of my fingers. This very thing had been fashioned by brown hands—who could tell how long ago?—and fitted to the end of a shaft. That was the hard stone fact my fingers were tampering with. In all likelihood, mine were the first hands to have touched it since then, the first white hands ever. Something was being imparted from the stone to me, some particular medicine. I felt more alive.

When I reached the truck, I held the arrowhead up to the light—a wide triangle of salmon-colored chert, streaked, especially at the point, with a vein of deeper red. Its maker, I supposed, would have used the tine of an antler; struck in the right place, the chunk of chert had sheared along anticipated lines. I liked the way it lay flat and light against my palm. Everything about it meant business.

Jay was vexed when I showed it to him, not because I had it and he didn't, but because he had walked right by it, almost stepped over it, without seeing it. It looked like a Savannah River stemmed projectile point, he said, but because of its size he thought it might be a cutting tool rather than an arrowhead. In either case, he was sure it was Stallings Island. None of that made sense to me, so he explained that archaeologists recognize three general periods of aboriginal occupation in the Southeast. The Paleo-Indian Era is ice-age, sparsely represented in our part of the country by fluted, lanceolate spear points. The Meso-Indian Era, usually called Archaic, runs from around 8000 B.C. to 1000 B.C. The people of this period were hunter-gatherers who learned the use of the bow and arrow and the art of pottery making. Stallings Island, located in the Savannah River a few miles above Augusta, is one of the important archaeological sites for the late Archaic. The artifact I had found, Jay said, bore a strong resemblance to one of the types characteristic of the Stallings Island site; it is known to archaeologists as Savannah River stemmed projectile. Point or knife, the relic I'd found was probably at least four thousand years old. I felt its edges again. The artifact was contemporary with the Hebrew patriarchs, with Esau the hunter of Genesis; yet it remained as sharp as some knives I had used to dress deer. As a projectile point, it would certainly bring one down, and fixed to a short handle it would do nicely for gutting and skinning an animal. I had no trouble envisioning such a scene, right here in the shadow of the Savannah River swamp—lean, copper bodies, quick cuts, a few necessary words.

Suddenly, I felt a twinge of guilt. Jay, I realized, was the one who should have the artifact; it was his knowledge after all that had recognized the site. But I didn't want to give it to him. I know now that he would have refused it, but I was not sure enough of that at the time to risk the offer. Finding an arrowhead had been important to me since childhood. I had one now—a good one—and I meant to keep it.

Whenever Henry Thoreau found an arrowhead, it gave him the feeling that it had been shot by an Indian from some past age straight into his own day, intended for him. "Surely," he wrote in his *Journal*, "their use was not so much to bear its fate to some bird or quadruped, or man, as it was to lie here near the surface of the earth for a perpetual reminder to the generations that come after." But a reminder of what, if not the obvious fact that they were made for killing—birds and quadrupeds, even invading white men? That's what mine reminded me of. Plain and unadorned, it proved to me the predacious history of our kind. I felt that what I was holding was human nature itself, fossilized.

From then on, it became my practice to spend Sunday mornings at the hunting camp looking for relics. They were not as hard to find as I had expected. As soon as I located a few good sites, I was almost always able to find at least one and often two or three. At the same time, I began to read about Indians, particularly Stoltman's monograph, *Groton Plantation,* and Charles Hudson's indispensable study, *The Southeastern Indians*. The earliest date for prehistoric occupation in the lower Savannah Valley that Stoltman had been able to establish was about 3000 B.C., or late Archaic. Yet one Sunday morning I found, lying in the furrow of a field, a beautiful lanceolate point, four inches long and milky blue; University of Georgia archaeologists identified it as Paleo-Indian, perhaps Folsom, circa 10,000 B.C.

Most of the relics I found were of the stemmed projectile type, but sometimes I found what my friend Freddie had called a bird point, in archaeological terminology a small triangular projectile point of the Yadkin type. According to Stoltman, these points were of the Neo-Indian Era, probably the Mississippian Culture that flourished here as late as the sixteenth century, when Hernando de Soto hacked his ruthless path through the southeastern part of the country.

When I returned home, I would place the arrowhead in an envelope, record the pertinent information, and then put the envelope into a drawer of my desk. Each time I did that I found myself wondering what arrowheads are good for now. As a reminder of the past, one should be enough, but I was filling up the drawer. Thoreau was not much help with that question, for he has little to say about collecting and keeping. The displays I had seen, those panels of artifacts mounted on green felt, had never held my attention, nor were my friends particularly interested in seeing the ones I had. The fact that I had found them in places where I hunted deer mattered only to me. Once or twice I had occasion to consider giving one to a friend or family member, but only the finest in my collection would have been good enough for that, and those were the ones I wanted to keep. So I kept them, had them, hoarded them. But they began to lose the power to please.

About that time a friend named Walter Cabin returned from an elk hunt in Montana. That was his first hunt in the northern Rockies, the dream of a lifetime come true, and he was eager to tell about it. Such a story, however, should not be blurted through a telephone or squeezed into five minutes between appointments. So Walter waited until we could sit down together with a glass of beer and attend to the telling as the story deserved.

An outfitter, he began, had dropped the party—Walter and three companions—at a camp deep in the Bob Marshall Wilderness. They had seven days to hunt. It took that long, Walter said, not only to learn the terrain and scout it but also to develop a sense of the behavior of local game that one has to have in order to hunt well. He awoke on the sixth day with confidence. By midday he was easing along a wooded shoulder near the top of a mountain. A hundred and fifty yards downhill he spied the blond rump patch of an elk, a cow, browsing among alders. Hoping that cow meant herd and herd meant bull, Walter took a position from which he could wait and watch. Soon, sure enough, he noticed the regular, almost methodical shaking of an alder top. A search through the scope revealed the tips of a rack. The bull was rubbing his antlers, but the brush was too heavy for Walter to see the body of the animal. A long wait followed. Finally, convinced that the bull was not going to move of his own accord into an open corridor, Walter risked a series of cow calls. The bull heard, listened for a moment, then resumed his rubbing. Walter called again. Again the bull stopped for an instant and listened. This conversation continued for a long time. Finally the bull gave in to curiosity and began to move uphill toward the corridor. But he stopped in heavy brush at the edge, still a hundred and twenty yards away. Leaves screened the target, but Walter found a hole and through it a patch of hair. The marksmanship he had developed as a boy shooting squirrels in West Virginia paid off. The elk lunged uphill, across the corridor, and collapsed upon a lodgepole log in a carpet of moss.

It took Walter an hour to roll the huge animal from the log into a position for field dressing. By the time he finished, the sky had clouded over and the light was beginning to fail. Knowing that he would not have time to butcher and pack out the meat before dark, he devoted himself to removing the head and cape. The night would be cold enough to keep the meat from spoiling.

Walter Cabin is lean and tall. I could see him clearly with the trophy on his shoulders, his head framed by the royal tines. Bowed beneath that weight, he started down the mountain. Before he reached camp, it began to snow—big wet flakes, he said, as big as silver dollars in the growing dark. With his eyes fixed on the trail before his feet, he came upon an arrowhead, white against the black organic soil. Using his rifle as a crutch, he managed to get down on one knee—the appropriate position, he said, for receiving such a gift. "I didn't even look at it then," he told me; "just dropped it in my pocket and kept on going."

Now in the dim light of the restaurant he took it from his pocket and showed it to me. It was a small hunting point but, driven by a strong bow, adequate even for elk, I supposed. As I held it up to the light, Walter said that he would probably give it to his son.

Because of the value I placed upon arrowheads—especially upon finding one under such circumstances—I was surprised that Walter was willing to give this one away, even to his son. But as I returned it to him, something in his demeanor, a composure in his heavy features, authenticated the gesture and made me think.

To stalk and kill an animal whose flesh becomes food is to participate in a mystery, whether the hunter knows it or not. Walter Cabin knew that. For him the taking of game was sacramental. He came off that mountain with the rack of his first elk on his shoulders, but the weight he was bearing was that of consciousness, and the weary trudge of his feet was a dance of gratitude. When the arrowhead appeared—occurred—in the trail before him, Walter knew it was part of the mystery, a concentration of all of the elements of the hunt—mountain, light, snow, and blood—granted by the red gods not as a mere souvenir but as a token affirming his kinship with all who had ever hunted wapiti in that high country.

As he knelt to pick it up, he must have known that the joy of the arrowhead was in the finding of it. He could no more keep that than he could the hunt itself, which the arrowhead signified and blessed. But by giving it to his son, also a hunter, Walter would invest the token with new meaning—increase its weight, you might say—and so sustain its power. The arrowheads I had tucked away in the dark drawer of my desk seemed sterile by comparison, bereft of the medicine that blesses. But perhaps it was not too late to redeem them. I would not give them away all at once or indiscriminately, but when a situation presented itself, I would be prepared.

The next time I went to the hunting camp I took a couple with me, just in case. The occasion was the annual November deer hunt hosted by a friend named Billy Claypoole. The first cold front of the fall had come through that week, stirring up the deer. By Saturday night the weather had begun to turn warm and rainy again, but everyone in camp had brought down game. Except me. There had been a time when such failure would have ruined my weekend, but I was experienced enough by then to accept the vagaries of the hunt. So I settled in at the supper table and looked forward to hearing the others tell their stories.

The telling had actually commenced two hours before, spontaneous and piecemeal, as hunters came in from the woods. With random groups of two or three it had drifted from the tailgates into the cabin and on back to the bunkhouse. Now, with supper over, it was about to be organized, ordered by the seating arrangement around the long pine table, directed by Billy. Part of his purpose in requiring each successful hunter to tell his story was to impress upon the three boys in camp the right way of talking about a hunt and to insure for them an opportunity to tell their own stories. Before such a group one was less likely to boast; the story might then become a means by which the hunter could discover, for both himself and his audience, something of the mystery of the thing he had done.

One of the boys was my son John, already at eighteen a veteran of the hunt and the supper-table talk but, for all that, laconic in his telling of a tale. He had killed a good cowhorn spike that morning, still-hunting in the swamp. When called on, he replied as though he were talking only to Billy, as though the rest of us weren't there. "I turned off the Don Terry Trail where it bends back to the north and started up that little slough in there, and the buck stepped out in front of me, right where Daddy said it would."

"Where *who* said it would?" Billy grinned.

I had taken some kidding that night for my lack of success, and John had heard it. With a quick glint of a smile he said, "My father."

Billy smiled. He and I had grown close through ten years of hunting together, but in spite of all the time we had spent in the woods, I had never come to regard myself as his peer. In the woods he had no peer. Some members of the club attributed his deep knowledge of wild things to his Indian blood. He didn't have much—a little Choctaw, I think—but what there was of it asserted itself in his features, his black eyes, and straight black Indian hair. When he came in from the woods with game, especially at times when no one else in camp killed anything, people would say, with grudging good humor, "Damn Indian."

It was Billy's habit in telling about a hunt always to direct attention from himself to the animal; no game was too insignificant for his appreciation, and the story was his way of paying tribute. But the buck he had killed that afternoon was small; most hunters would have been embarrassed to acknowledge it. It was certainly legal, a legitimate spike buck, but borderline for someone of Billy's skill and experience. Easy to kill, such deer provide excellent meat for the table but poor material for stories. I was waiting to see how Billy was going to tell about this one.

What he did was call on me. "How 'bout it, Jim? You have a story for us?"

Could he have actually forgotten, I wondered, that I had not killed a deer? Then it hit me. He knew, all right. He was just forcing me to make a public confession of my failure. Okay. I could handle that. It was a bit below the belt, but without malice. Just a part of the evening's entertainment, at my expense.

"John's already told what little bit of a story I had. What we want to hear about is your buck."

Billy acknowledged the finesse of that response with an almost imperceptible smile. "There's not that much to tell, really. It *was* a beautiful little hunt. I love a drizzle, like it was about dark, so I was easing through those young pines up there in Jack Hill Woods, sort of checking out those long openings, more or less just enjoying the afternoon. Then I saw this deer. He was standing out there—maybe seventy-five yards— in those scattered pines, and I could just barely see him because he was standing in broomsedge up to his shoulders."

"It's not like he was the biggest buck you ever saw," someone teased.

Billy ignored him. "Y'all remember how that fog came in right at dark? I couldn't make out any antlers at all, but I had a feeling it was a buck. I looked away just long enough to wipe off my bi-nocs, and when I looked again—I mean half a second later—he was gone. It was like he just dematerialized. That's about the only time I can think of—hunting deer, I mean—when I've been totally faked out."

"So I was just standing there, looking down, sort of scratching my head, I guess, and right between my feet I saw an arrowhead, a beautiful little bird point right between my feet. I didn't want to pick it up—I mean it just looked like it was exactly where it was supposed to be, like it belonged right there. But then I started thinking about the Indian that made it and what he would have done in that situation. And I figured I needed some of his medicine, so I picked it up and put it in my pocket and stood there sort of rubbing it between my thumb and finger, and all of a sudden it came to me what that little buck had done—he had bedded down, right in his tracks. It made sense. He had probably caught a whiff of me, but the wind confused him. He didn't know where I was, but he sure knew where I wasn't. So he said, 'I better ease down right here.' I knew that was exactly what had happened. I slipped up through those pines, and, sure enough, I saw those two little spikes"—Billy held his fists together and raised his index fingers—"shining in the wet broomsedge."

Billy produced the arrowhead and held it up for the table to see. It was white with a concave base, long and narrow for a bird point and, against the glow of the lantern overhead, translucent.

"It wasn't the Hartford stag," he continued, "but it was a beautiful little hunt. And I'd like to present this arrowhead to the gentleman on my right."

Billy handed it to me.

My first impulse was to refuse it, as his had been to leave it on the ground. But he had picked it up, and the arrowhead belonged to him; it would not stop being his by my accepting it. Then I saw that Billy had chosen this way to bring me into the circle of storytellers—by inviting me to share his hunt he was acknowledging before the others my right as a hunter to be there. If I had declined that gift, it would have crumbled to ash in Billy's hand. So I reached for it, and Billy made it easy: "Besides," he said, "I know how he'd covet it if I didn't."

The table laughed as I took the bird point. It was as thin as a Moravian wafer. As I ran my nail along its fine serrations, its medicine worked again and I remembered the best thing I had ever heard about arrowheads. When the others got quiet, I told them that I knew a man named Mac who used to hunt for arrowheads in Texas; Mac had told me about running into an old fellow out there who looked at what Mac had found and said, "People think it was Indians made them things, but it weren't Indians—it was God. He took and strewn the earth with 'em. The Indians might have used them when they found them, but they didn't make them." Mac had said that the old man never cracked a smile, so I told it to them straight, just the way I'd heard it.

MOUNTAIN SPIRITS

THE MAN who told me how to find Bascomb Creek had lowered his voice to keep from being overheard by the people standing near us. "It's hard to find but it's easy to fish," he'd whispered, "and it's jumping with trout. Just keep it to yourself." That sounded too good to be true, but as soon as I got home, I called my friend Charlie Creedmore. At five o'clock the following Saturday morning we were driving north toward Rabun County. At first light we crossed the concrete bridge over Bascomb Creek, pulled over at a wide spot in the gravel road, and climbed out. Charlie headed upstream while I made my way south through the dim woods. After walking for perhaps twenty minutes, I stepped into the water and began fishing back toward the bridge. My skepticism had been well-founded. The canopy was too low for easy casting, and because of drought the water was warm and shallow, the pools few and far between. I waded fast, anxious for a pool I could cast to, and before I knew it I was back at the bridge. It was not yet eight o'clock.

Between me and the bridge, and several terraces above my head, lay a wide, inviting pool. Streams of water spilled from it, splashing down to where I stood. I climbed slowly, careful not to spook any fish it might hold. Then, at eye level, on shelved stone around the pool, I saw the trash: Styrofoam fast-food containers, empty cans labeled niblets corn, beer cans and the plastic six-pack rings they had come in. I could almost see the crowd that left it, craning their necks at the hatchery truck on the bridge above, eager for its bounty of washed-out rainbows. Keep it to yourself, the man had said.

At least a dozen trout had survived the last onslaught. They were schooled near the bottom—eight- and ten-inchers they looked like—hanging still in the cold lower layer. Tin cans glinted through the depths.

I congratulated myself a little on having the decency not to cast to those harried fish, though in fact I doubted that they would take a fly. I thought of the thermos of coffee in the Blazer, said to hell with fishing, and climbed through the littered woods toward the road. Near the top I came upon a blind TV, upright among the hemlocks. The road itself looked like a garbage dump. I laid my flyrod across the hood of the Blazer and poured a cup of coffee. Amidst the trash across the road fluttered strips of toilet paper.

I did not want to think that mountain people had made this mess. I wanted to believe that mountain people behaved like the stout old craftsmen I had read about in the Foxfire books, that treasure of Appalachian lore collected right here in Rabun County by Eliot Wigginton and his high school students. I knew better than that, of course. From what I'd seen out on 441—souvenir shops with names like Houn' Dawg and Kountry Korner, fast-food chains, convenience stores—it was clear that progress had come to the mountains.

During my first year at the university I had taught a young man who had been part of Wigginton's first group. It may have been from him that I learned of the Foxfire project. I remembered well a quart jar of white likker he brought me one Monday morning. "That's what they call it," he said. "White likker. And that right there is the best in Rabun County."

The jar had lasted three years because I drank it slowly, saving it for those times when I needed an antidote against the banalities of the world I lived in.

I turned to look again at the broken TV in the woods. Its doleful stare from out of the hemlocks reminded me of a colleague who lost his composure one day over the stupidity of a program his children were watching. Before his rage spent itself, he had hauled the family set out into the country and shot it to pieces with a deer rifle. He had been a little embarrassed after the fact, but he explained to me that he'd had to do it, had to accomplish its destruction with his own hands. In the long run, though, it did no good. By the time he got back home, a neighbor, having heard that his children were deprived of television, had donated one of hers.

I at such times just took a ritual sip from the fruit jar. The bite of that mountain corn—like good medicine—reminded me that in Rabun County at least people were still living in a world crafted by their own hands. But that had been fifteen years ago; the jar was long since empty, and I had not tasted any since. The man who made it was probably dead by now, his sons buying whiskey at the store.

As I began to unseat the reel from my flyrod, I heard a car coming, tires on gravel, approaching the bridge. But it wasn't a car. It was an old pickup, dead-paint blue, and it pulled to a stop directly across the road from me, scattering trash. I became uncomfortably conscious of my flyfishing vest, Orvis zingers dangling down the front, laminated landing net hanging from the back. I wished I had taken it off. I ignored the truck, intent on the rod.

A door opened, slammed shut. Someone was coming. I glanced—a local it was, sleeveless shirt unbuttoned, black hair greased down solid. Thick glasses magnified his eyes, but the detail that bothered me most was the frames—opaque green and plastic-looking, dime-store glasses. I had often berated city folks ignorant enough to assume that everyone in Rabun County is as depraved as the two perverts in James Dickey's

Deliverance, but this fellow at best looked like the kind who would dump his broken TV in the woods. I wondered where Charlie was, what was taking him so long. The man was not walking straight toward me so much as sidling in my direction, and while his face was set my way, his eyes seemed fixed, sure enough, on the television set behind me. A bad burn was healing on the back of one hand.

"You going or coming?" he asked.

"Just waiting on my buddy," I said.

"What you fishing with?"

For the first time in my life I hated having to say flyrod.

The man glanced at it, muttered an obscenity.

"I couldn't do nothing with 'em," I said. "Y'all getting ready to try 'em?"

"You ever hear about old Towse?"

The senselessness of the question disturbed me more than anything yet. "No," I said, "I don't believe I have." I unjointed the sections of my rod, anxious for Charlie.

"I thought you might have heared about old Towse."

The man was close enough now for me to smell the whiskey on his breath. I had a feeling that a lot depended on the answer I gave. "No. You'll have to tell me about him."

"Coon dog. You want a drink?"

As early as it was, I chose what seemed the prudent course. "I believe I might."

The man led me across the road. As we approached the pickup, he spoke to his companion, who was concealed behind the glare of the windshield. "Monroe, reach me that bottle."

While Monroe was bestirring himself, I noticed a revolver on the dash—an unholstered nickel thirty-eight, every visible chamber loaded. I could imagine it sliding hard from one side to the other as the truck swung through hairpin curves.

Monroe climbed out on the far side—an older man with

a puffy, pocked face, wearing overalls and a soft-looking old baseball cap. Without a word or nod of greeting he offered the bottle across the hood—an old vodka bottle from the looks of what was left of the label, and the liquid it contained was vodka-clear. A blue and red can of RC Cola followed.

Moonshine can range from superb to poisonous. I had no idea what I was on the verge of tasting. But as afraid as I was to drink it, I was more afraid not to. Besides, I wanted to hear the story. If this homemade product fell short of my memory of the student's gift, I would say, "That's good, thank you, but I'm afraid it's a little early in the day for me."

It was good. I mean it tasted right as far as I could tell, serious but smooth, no barbed wire in it, and a flavor unlike that of any commercial sourmash I had ever drunk. I declined the RC and took another swallow.

"They's a Church a God preacher over in Walhally put out a bluegrass song on him," the one with glasses said.

On Towse, he meant.

"And they tell me a feller up in Franklin made a ballad about him too, but I ain't heared that one."

"Can you sing the Church of God one?" I asked.

"I ain't got my guitar. You remember the words to it, Monroe?"

"I can't keep 'em straight."

"Damn if he won't a good one. Trail didn't get too cold for Towse."

"I didn't think there were that many coons up here."

"It ain't. Not like it used to be. Where you from?"

I told them I lived in Athens. The one with glasses, whose name was Roy, said they used to hunt around Athens—down in Jackson County—a world of coons down there. He asked was I with the university. Somewhat surprised, I said yes. He figured that must be a good job. Monroe said a cousin of his had a daughter went to the university, he thought I might have known her, named Tami Bascomb, works for a bank in Atlanta now. I started to explain that the university was much larger than most people realized, but Roy passed me the bottle and Monroe said, "They ain't near the game in these mountains they used to be."

I was aware that the chestnut blight, by removing a primary source of food, had contributed to the extirpation of deer and turkeys, but I also knew that recent restocking programs had been successful. "I thought the deer and turkeys were coming back," I said.

"Too much goddam Atlanta," Monroe said. "Used to, a man could feed his family just on hunting and fishing, plant a garden, maybe run a little likker on the side. Right up yonder in that cove one day I killed four pheasants and thirteen gray squirrels."

"Is that right?" I asked, careful to conceal my skepticism. By pheasant Monroe meant ruffed grouse. I had hunted the bird enough to know that four in one day, in these steep, wooded hills, required a combination of remarkable luck and exceptional wing shooting.

"Shore did. Shot three on the ground and one in the air. And thirteen gray squirrels." Monroe held his fist to his face. "I had me a string of stuff this long."

"The thing about Towse," Roy said, "he wouldn't give up on no coon. You take a normal dog, a old coon'll lose him, swim the river on him, run on rock—rock'll not hold his scent, see. But Towse'd stay on his ass—rock, water, what have you. He run a coon one night up in a rock clift." Roy took a pull on the bottle, chased it with RC, passed the bottle to me. "That's what done him in."

I had to ask Roy to explain what he meant by a rock clift.

"Why, it's kindly like a hole."

"A hole in the ground?"

"No. It's where you have a clift in the rock." He paused, then continued, "Hell, it's just a rock clift, is what it is."

I featured a deep cleft in the face of a cliff. "And Towse did what? Ran a coon into the rock clift?"

"That he did. Time we got there, the hole was done caved in, all them dogs a-running round, a-climbing rocks, barking treed. My brother said, 'I don't see Towse.' The old man said, ' 'Cause he's in there with 'at coon is why.' You remember that, Monroe? And shore 'nough, you could hear him; over all them other dogs, you could hear him way down in that rock clift, a-killing that coon."

Somewhere in Roy's account Monroe had begun to talk. Intent on Roy, I had picked up only snatches, enough to realize that his comments had nothing to do with Towse. He was talking about fishing as far as I could tell, but Roy seemed not to mind; he didn't even slow up. The two men were as oblivious to each other as two radios tuned to different stations, turned up loud. It was frustrating to try to hear what both were saying. If I could stop Monroe with a question, maybe Roy could finish his story. "*What* kind of trout?" I asked.

"Speckled trout."

Roy was saying something about the cave-in, something to do with a slab-sided bitch that was down in there with Towse, but Monroe went right on. "Damn near rare as a chestnut tree any more. Hatchery fish is what done it. Used to, speckled trout was all you'd catch."

Roy was still talking—not competing with Monroe, just telling his story. But I was interested also in this mysterious speckled trout. "I'm not familiar with that fish," I said.

"Generally he'll not go more'n six inches. And real bright. Orange and red and black and white and speckled."

"You mean a brook trout?"

"No. A speckled trout. Old-timey, original fish. Catch him in the morning, he'll not rot on you like these here goddam stocked fish. He's the best eating fish they is. Meat's right pink. I caught forty-three one day, on up Bascomb Creek here."

Roy had stopped to take a drink and had not yet recovered his voice.

"What did you catch them on?" I asked, thinking corn, probably.

"Sawyers. Sawyers and waust grubs."

I had to ask what he meant by sawyers.

"Fat white worms. You find 'em in a old rotten log. Best bait they is. That and waust and hornet grubs."

I wondered how one acquired wasp and hornet larvae, especially during the summer when nests are active, but Monroe seemed not to regard that as a matter requiring explanation.

"You need to cook 'em first. Bake 'em in the oven about forty-five minutes, get 'em right tough. That way they'll stay on your hook. Used to, it'd take my daddy three days to get ready to go a-fishing, three days to gather up his bait. But when he went he by god caught 'em. All speckled trout too.

"It's best to wait for a good hard pour to dinge-y up the creek. It come up a hell of a rain the day I caught them forty-three. I found me a stooping tree to get up under and waited for it to quit. Time it did I caught the fire out of 'em."

"Was Bascomb Creek named after some of your people?"

"I imagine it was, but I couldn't tell you just exactly who. My granddaddy owned from the bridge here clear up to the headwaters on Hogpen Mountain. But it was Bascomb Creek before his time. They used to be a world of Bascombs all up through here. I reckon we was all kin one way or another."

"Did your granddaddy sell his land to the Forest Service?"

"A right smart of it, he did. And what little bit the government left, goddam developers got. You know Blue Mountain

Ski Resort? Got that off my granddaddy's old sister and her not knowing no better."

"It's got to where now a man can't afford to keep his own place," Roy said.

I was afraid the end of his story about Towse had been swallowed up in Monroe's lament for speckled trout, as the dog himself was buried beneath the rock slide. But surely there was more to it than just a dead coon hound, or why would Roy have asked a stranger if he'd heard about old Towse? That might have been the whiskey, of course, but people didn't make ballads out of what I'd heard so far.

"Goddam Atlanta," Monroe said.

"Florida too," Roy added.

"They say these tourists spend a lot of money up here," I suggested.

"Shit." For once they spoke in unison. Roy said he was yet to see the first green dollar of it hisself, and Monroe said, "You want to see that tourist money, look at all this trash strowed up and down the road. People got no self-respect."

I did not believe that tourists from Atlanta and Florida had driven through the National Forest throwing garbage from their windows, and I didn't think Monroe did either, but somewhere in his comment was an association of one with the other that was worth thinking about.

"Same thing with likker. Used to, a man took pride in making whiskey, but this goddam radiator likker they're selling now will kill you. I've seen some would peel the paint off a car. They was a fellow up here at Scaly one night spit out a mouthful against the door of a pickup truck, it run down the side, took the paint right with it."

"How do they use a radiator?"

"Condenser. Instead of a worm. Then they'll put potash in on you, Irish taters, no damn telling what all. Possum fall in and drown, they don't give a damn, run it anyway. I'd not touch a drop that I didn't know who made it. Not like it is now."

I was somewhat comforted by Monroe's implicit endorsement of the product we were drinking. "I guess you know who made this then?"

Monroe paused for a second. Then he said, "Yeah, I do."

"I wasn't asking who. I'm just glad you know it's good."

"I guaran-goddam-tee it's good," Roy said. "This here ain't nothing but pure corn." He thumped the bottom of the bottle to make it bead. "Same as it's always been."

"I guess y'all's ancestors must have passed it down—the right way to make it, I mean—father to son."

Roy said, "That they did."

He took a swallow. "The bitch come out after four days. We thought it was her that caused the slide—"

"Generally is," Monroe interjected.

"—She was a slab-sided bitch to start with, and after four days in that hole she was poor enough to squeeze through. But Towse was too stout through the shoulders."

"What kind of dog was he?"

"Half redbone and half bluetick and half bulldog. Eighteen days in that hole, he was, and him without nothing but that coon to eat. We like to never got him out."

"What did you do? Dig him out?"

"Blowed him out with dynamite. Case and a half, quarter stick at a time."

I accepted the exaggeration as an appropriate tribute to the dog. I accepted it as I accepted their whiskey, with pleasure. "Good Lord. How much rock did you have to blast through?"

"Forty foot."

"And he was still alive."

"Just barely. You remember when he come up out of there, Monroe? All bowed up and caved in, he was, but he by god walked out on his own. 'Course he never heared too good after that. My daddy just retired him, let him lay up by the stove for as long as he lived, which won't but about another year. But he was one more tough son of a bitch in his prime, won't he, Monroe?"

"He was that. How old was you when your daddy started you at his still?"

"Had me toting jars when I was eight."

It crossed my mind to wonder if Roy's people might have been the ones who had made the whiskey the student had brought me years before. I told them about that—"the best in Rabun County"—and admitted that I'd been curious ever since about the way it was made.

For the first time that morning Monroe laughed. "Why? You ain't aiming to start one up your own self, are you?"

Before I could answer, Roy took over. "Whiskey ain't something you can just lay out the making of like you can a house and expect somebody to come along and read how and then do it. It takes a man that respects corn to do it right. Corn's got its own nature, see. You run it before its time, before them old dogheads go to rising, or run it too fast or cook it too hot, why it'll not be fit to drink. Making whiskey's more a matter of caring how good instead of how much. A man that don't plan to drink his own likker, I damn shore don't want none of it myself."

"You drink it right," Monroe said, "good likker'll not hurt you. Drink all you want, get up the next morning, eat what they put before you, sausage and eggs and cathead biscuits. I know a preacher drinks it. He don't what you'd call regular drink now, but he will take a sup or two of an evening. Says it makes him rest better. You want some more?"

I decided Charlie could drive us back to Athens.

"They's a Church a God preacher over here to Walhally

made up a bluegrass song about old Towse," Roy said. "Put it out on a record. He deserved it too. He was a uncommon dog."

Charlie came walking out of the woods not long after that, as disappointed in Bascomb Creek as I had been. The bottle was almost empty, but we hung around the front end of Roy's pickup long enough for him to have a taste. I asked if they could sell me a bottle to take home, but they said no, the one we'd drunk was all they had.

I rode back to Athens as high on Roy's story as I was on his whiskey. To make the story mine, I tried to tell it to Charlie while Roy's words still sang in my head, but it didn't work. In my telling, the story went flat—just another Old Blue tale with appropriate exaggeration. Then it hit me: To tell it right you had to have someone to do Monroe's part. For the two men had been telling the same story all along—I could see it now—two men with nothing better to do that morning than hang around the hood of a pickup truck with a fifth of white likker in a recycled vodka bottle and an audience who must have looked to them like he might need to hear what they had to tell.

COMING OFF THE BACK
OF BRASSTOWN BALD

EVEN WHEN he was married, Billy Claypoole was subject to impulses that drove him from home, down the blacktop county roads through the waning afternoons, into the night. Sometimes he stopped at my house, unannounced, wanting me to go with him.

Looking back after ten years, I'm more impressed now by my wife's forbearance than I was then. Occasionally Billy surprised us in the late afternoon, when she was cooking supper, sometimes on Saturday morning, just in time to save me from a weekend of yard work. I'm sure she was not happy about my riding off in that blue Blazer, but she could have made it harder than she did. The time I'm thinking about now, Billy was unmarried, which may have caused Jane to feel a little apprehensive. She asked when I expected to be back. I said, "Don't you know I can't answer that? Before Sunday morning." Well, she certainly hoped so. We had a Sunday-school party Saturday night, she reminded me, nonoptional.

Billy and I camped that night beside a trout stream up near the North Carolina line. In the long summer twilight we each caught a limit of rainbow trout, none too long to fit into a skillet, and killed two apiece for supper. Billy had packed a measure of flour, some cooking oil, coffee, and one Vidalia onion. While I cleaned fish, he gathered from a nearby garden (owned by a friend) eggplant, tomatoes, green beans, and squash. We used a cooler for a table and ate by the light of the fire, which felt good after the sun went down. It was even chillier at first light, the meadow cobwebbed with dew. By the time Billy had a pot of coffee perking, I had caught three fish for breakfast. By ten we were packed and on our way, though not toward home.

Billy liked to stop at roadside produce stands and at country stores where old men sit around debating the distances to towns stamped on the bottoms of their Coca-Cola bottles, and he loved to drive down unpaved mountain roads that he'd never driven before. That was fine with me. I could spread out in that Blazer, grab something to drink from the cooler, and listen to Merle Haggard sing desperado songs while Billy did the driving. That morning the cool mountain air shimmered with sunlight; I punched in a George Jones tape and we still had Jimmy Buffett to go.

A sign on the highway announced the turnoff to Brasstown Bald—at 4,784 feet the highest peak in Georgia. Billy flipped his turn signal.

I couldn't see why he wanted to do that. The only attraction, besides ravens, was an observation tower from which you can see what they say are four, or maybe five, states—a blue panorama of peaks and valleys growing fainter in all directions, fading into haze. The views from Tray and Blood are just as spectacular, and since you have to earn the vantage point by a sweaty climb, that much better. The slightly greater altitude of Brasstown is just a number, as poor an excuse for a trip to the top as December 31 is for getting drunk. Ravens, on the other hand, could make the trip worthwhile. Though considered a trash bird out west, that scavenger is rare in Georgia, occurring, like heavy snow, only at higher elevations. As serious Georgia birdwatchers know, the parking lot on Brasstown Bald is a likely place to find them.

Maybe we'll see ravens, I thought.

We did—one bird—a blowsy, outsize crow, working the parking lot for tourist trash. That and three or four empty automobiles that, having gone as far as they could, were waiting for the shuttle to return their owners from the peak. Billy stopped. The raven ignored us. Then, swinging suddenly through a wide turn, he said, "I want to show you something." With that we bumped over a curb and headed into woods.

I knew better than to ask. It was Billy's way to forgo the banked four-lane, or any beaten path. In the years that I had known him he had walked away from the security of an academic appointment, gotten a divorce, and sold his house in the suburbs. He was now exploring uncharted ground, and I, on temporary vacation from cutting grass and pruning shrubs, had come along for the ride.

From the random woods we came suddenly into a sunken lane, an ancient roadbed cobbled with natural stone. Now we're headed somewhere, I thought. The sense of purpose was a comfort. Billy must have been here before, must know that the road leads to something I would like to see—a long-abandoned resort hotel, tumbling down the mountain, or a wet rock face inscribed with petroglyphs, or a jutting boulder with a brass plaque saying that here some Cherokee chief once stood, looking out over his domain.

How Billy knew of such places baffled me. A native of Alabama, he had not come to Georgia until after I did. Yet he had taken me to forgotten shrines throughout the mountains and the Piedmont, out-of-the-way places such as a meadow in the midst of the Oglethorpe County woods that the eighteenth-century traveler William Bartram described as a buffalo lick, or the Kettle Creek battleground, where patriots under Andrew Pickens drove the Tories from the upper Savannah River. We heard a turkey gobble from there one evening.

The road we were taking down the mountain could have

been the original trail to the top of Brasstown, an artifact of people's longing to ascend, of hunters' quests for more elusive game, and later of settlers' needs for timber—chestnut and walnut for furniture, the straight trunks of poplar for houses and barns. Cut through topsoil down to corrugated bedrock, the road ran deeper than the ground on either side, walled by ferny banks that brushed the fenders of the Blazer as we forged ahead. The aroma of white pine and hemlock spiced the air. Rounding a bend, we surprised a ruffed grouse, a rufous male. Billy stopped. The grouse strutted away from us, nervous, then whirred out of sight.

Out of the green woods, we descended in switchbacks, the road rougher now, badly rutted on the left side so that the Blazer rode canted, forcing me to brace myself to keep from sliding into the driver's seat. As high off the ground as the vehicle sat, its underside kept scraping rock. I was tense from watching for a spot wide enough for us to turn around. Much farther, at the rate the road was deteriorating, and we would have gone too far. Not even rangers, as far as I could tell, had come this way in a long time.

Busy with the steering wheel, Billy said, "See if you can find that Buffett tape that has the one on it about attitudes and latitudes."

Jimmy Buffett should write a song about Billy, I thought.

"Is it afternoon yet?" he asked.

I said it was, had been for a while.

"Then why aren't we drinking a beer?"

I took two cans from the ice in the cooler.

"I ever tell you about the time I saw the black-necked stilts?" I asked.

He couldn't remember.

"About ten years ago. We were staying on Hilton Head. We'd been to Savannah that day, and a birdwatcher I knew told me that a flock of stilts was hanging around a borrow pit just across the Savannah River Bridge. Have you ever seen one?"

"In Florida."

"Well, I never had, and I'd been looking for them for years. So on the way back, late in the afternoon and hot as hell, everybody tired, I turned off the highway where Tom had said, and there was this sign: Men at work, KEEP OUT. But you know how birdwatchers are. If Tom had done it, I didn't see why I couldn't.

"I don't know what they were doing—dredging, I guess— but all that land along the South Carolina side looked like the Sahara desert, just a wide expanse of sand, and way off in the distance you could see where they had left their bulldozers and draglines.

"In the family station wagon, now—hungry children, tired wife and all—I drove right up to the borrow pit, and sure enough there were the stilts, right where Tom had said they'd be—that black-and-white pattern so startling among the duller shorebirds, and you could see their dark red legs reflected in the water. And there were avocets too, just like they're supposed to be with stilts. Now that I had them nailed down, I decided to come back the next day, when I could take my time. So I backed around. The sand looked firm, hard-packed. But the second I backed out of the ruts I sank to my axle. And there we were, way to hell off in the middle of nowhere, tired and hot and hungry, and the children starting to cry. That's why it makes me nervous to leave the main roads, especially in a car full of people who are depending on me to get them home."

"But you saw the stilts."

"Are you interested in hearing how I got out?"

"I figured that was coming next."

"Through the binoculars I could see a bunch of guys standing around the bulldozers so I set out—a half mile across that open sand, the sun hanging low and red behind me—while they stood around wondering what the hell I was doing out there to begin with. The last thing I wanted to do was tell them bird-watching. There were eight or ten of them, black and white, knocked off and drinking beer, lounging in the heat waves of those machines. It's hard to announce to a whole group that you need help, especially when you don't know who is in charge, but I didn't have much selection, as Marlon Brando says.

"One of them spoke up, 'That your car out yonder?'

" 'I was hoping I could get somebody to give me a push.'

"Nothing, not a word, just left me hanging there. Finally, somebody said, 'Larry?' or whatever his name was.

"Larry was this lanky white fellow, T-shirt and Caterpillar hat, heavy mustache. 'I don't know,' he said. 'Howard?'

"This black guy spoke up then, said, 'What you doing out here?'

"I could see that he was the man I needed to talk to, but I couldn't think of anything to tell him but the truth.

" 'Birdwatching.'

"The rest of them eased forward just a little. You could tell this was the high point of their day. Howard said, 'Birdwatch-ing?' I can't say it the way he did, but the tone he used was the reason I hadn't wanted to have to tell them.

" 'You didn't see that sign up there on the highway?'

"I explained about Tom's directions and said I figured any-body working down here would have been gone by now.

"Howard said, 'I imagine you glad we weren't.'

"I said I sho was.

" 'Larry,' he said, 'go on over there and see can you get him out.'

"Larry climbed up on this big D-8 and I found a place to sit somewhere and we went tractoring back to the car. He scooped me out with his blade."

By the time I finished the story we had gone too far to back out, and I had despaired of a place to turn around. Billy was driving too fast, despite my feet planted hard against the floorboard. With a wall of mountain on our right, he swung through the curves, blind to what lay beyond. Off to the left I could see through openings in the foliage blue depths of valley. We had come a long way, it seemed, yet still the bottom of the mountain was far below.

The first obstacle was a fallen tree—a huge hemlock—lying across the road. With its roots clinging to the hillside on the right, the massive trunk rested upon limbs driven into the soil when it fell. Two limbs, in fact, vertical to the trunk's horizontal, framed a neat doorway. A Volkswagen would have made it through easily.

"Reckon we can ease through?" Billy asked.

"Looks right snug to me."

"Hold my beer," he said.

The Blazer nosed into the doorway and stopped.

"Get out and see if we're clear up top."

I did, but I couldn't tell. "If you hold your breath," I said.

The Blazer fit with no more than an inch of clearance. Billy stopped again when he was far enough through to open the door on his side and climb out. He retrieved his beer and stepped back. "Just about skin tight."

In two steps or three he climbed the front of the Blazer like a staircase, stepped up onto the roof, and sat on the trunk of the hemlock. I followed. It was a fine perch, a good place to drink a beer, but when I finished, I was ready to move on. If real trouble lay ahead, I wanted to confront it as soon as possible, but Billy was content to stay where we were for as long as it took to drink another can.

"Doesn't it say something in the Bible about strait is the gate and narrow the way?" he asked.

"Yeah," I said, "that leads up. We're going down."

"I thought that *was* the way up."

"I don't care which way it is as long as I get home by six."

"You remember *The Missouri Breaks,* where Marlon Brando asks that cowboy if he thinks life is like a mountain railway?"

Billy was referring to the scene in which the Brando character, a hired killer dressed like a preacher, sings the old gospel song "Mountain Railway." He's sitting by a campfire with a scared cowboy who has about decided that the clerical collar is a joke.

"Randy Quaid," I said. "And that's the best line in the movie: 'I don't think life's like nothing I've ever seen before,' he says."

Billy laughed. "Well that's what you sound like. You better drink another beer."

He climbed down to get it, fetching his camera at the same time; while I drank, he snapped a picture of me sitting on the tree trunk, my feet on top of the vehicle. Then he had me take a shot of him. After thirty minutes or so we piled back into the Blazer, and Billy eased on through the strait gate of hemlock.

One doesn't often run into young women in the woods. These two were toiling up the mountain, sweatshirts tied around their waists. Billy stopped and greeted them. Red-faced and sweaty, they were both sucking wind. When they had caught their breath, the heavier one asked how much farther it was to the top.

"Not too far," he said.

They grunted their relief at that good news.

"Y'all look like you could use a beer," Billy said.

They stepped back from the window, looked at each other, and grinned uncertain little grins. "Beer?"

"Coors in a can. Ice cold."

"We better not be drinking beer," they giggled.

"Well, that's the best we can do," Billy said. "What's it like from here on down?"

They rolled their eyes at each other. "Steep."

"I mean the road."

"Oh. The road's not all that bad. You ought to make it okay."

Under way again, I said, "You must have thought the truth would have been too hard on those girls."

"Well, it's *not* that far," Billy laughed, "not by Blazer anyway."

"Yeah, and they are having this same conversation right now: 'Well, it's not that bad, not by foot anyway.'"

"Relax," Billy said.

I tried to, easing up on the floorboard and reaching for another beer. A movie of us would have shown a big-footed four-wheel drive clomping down a rocky road, confident as could be, but mount a camera in the seat I occupied and the descent would take your breath. No sooner had I popped open the can when up ahead the road stopped. Just stopped in midair. "Oh shit," I said. We climbed out and took a look. A four-foot drop, at least, straight down. So much for the Sunday-school party, I thought. If we start walking now, maybe we can get to a telephone in time for me to call. Jane won't be happy, but it's not my fault.

"Okay," Billy said, but he was talking to himself.

"What do you mean 'okay'?"

By way of an answer he got back in the Blazer. I followed, wondering how many times I had done just that, having no idea what he planned next. He eased forward to the brink. Beyond the high front end of the vehicle I saw only space.

"I'm going to nose it over easy and slide on down. Just like we did that time at Groton."

We had been driving a woods road along the Savannah River, the time he was talking about, and come upon a rain-swollen slough that had washed out a culvert and cut a deep running channel across the road. I had gotten out, crossed on a log, and watched as Billy attempted to bring the Blazer through. We had killed game that morning, Billy two black hogs, I a hog and an antlered buck. After dragging the animals out, we had brought the Blazer around and picked them up, slinging all four, by ropes tied to their feet, from a tire mounted on the front of the vehicle—a barbaric spectacle in itself, but when that Blazer came surging up from the water, pointed toward the sky, with all those streaming beasts hanging from the tire, it was positively mythological.

"Hold on," he said, and over we went.

Between the keening of steel on stone, the hammering of metal parts, and the two ankle-breaking jolts as first the front and then the rear end struck, I was convinced that we had left our vital parts strewn upon the rocky staircase. But the Blazer lurched forward, both axles grinding.

"If those girls couldn't remember anything worse than that," Billy said, "we're in good shape."

Any hope I might have nursed of yet backing out, heroic though such a feat would have been, was gone now.

"I've been hunting and fishing and camping for fifteen years," I said. "With Walter and Jack and Charlie and Bob and Jim Meunier. Why is it that you're the only one who gets me into these situations?"

"We have had some good times, haven't we?"

"Now that we can look back on them."

"You're still not having fun?"

"I'm too busy looking forward to the time when we can look back on this trip."

"I don't know whether you'd consider Montana real life or not, but I was fishing out there a couple of years ago—have I told you this?"

"I don't know yet."

"Waist-deep in a strong current, trying to cast and keep my feet at the same time, and all of a sudden I looked up and there was this woman, right in front of me, sitting on a boulder, sunbathing."

"Nekkid, of course."

"No, she had on shorts."

"And you offered her a beer."

"Actually she was the one who had the beer. Moosehead, I think."

"Which she was more than happy to share, I'm sure."

"Caught a beautiful brown trout that morning too."

Suddenly the mountainside fell away so precipitously on our left that it looked as though we had entered the familiar cartoon road that runs between a steep wall and a sheer drop.

For no apparent reason Billy smiled. It had nothing to do with me, with anything I'd said, but was instead a spontaneous response to this new circumstance. I saw clearly then that this fool thing we were doing, this wild, uncertain choice, was not just for my benefit; Billy might well have come this way by himself. Risk was his natural habitat. Whether it was that realization or the beer or something else, I unlocked my knees and took my feet off the brakes. We weren't going to make it home by six now anyway. Since Billy had no curfew nor place he had to be, we might not make it back before tomorrow morning. I didn't even open my mouth when we came around a curve and ran smack up against a boulder—a slab the size of a sofa lying across the road.

"Looks like those girls would have remembered something like that," Billy said.

We climbed out again. Moving the rock was out of the question, but we had to give it a try, to test our strength against impossibility. More flat than round and higher on the end toward the wall at our right, the rock slanted dangerously toward the outer edge. We couldn't budge it.

"Back when I was in high school," I said, "a friend and I were trying to figure out a way to go to Europe for the summer. We were talking about it one night at a filling station—we'd stopped for gas—and this old boy who worked there said, 'What's the big deal? You got a car, ain't you?' My friend said, 'You ever heard of the Atlantic Ocean?' The old boy said, 'So what? Just drive around the son of a bitch.'"

"That's exactly what I'm fixing to do," Billy said. "Why don't you stand right here and sort of give me directions."

Before I could think of the best way to say what a good idea I thought that was, he was behind the wheel again. I stepped up onto the thick end of the slab, a good two feet high. To get the front tires up onto it, Billy would have to attack at the lower end, too close to the outer edge. Any vehicle, clambering across, would surely slide off.

Instead of backing up to get a running start as I expected, Billy crept forward, hugging the wall, toward the end that looked too high to climb; at the last moment he accelerated just enough to get up and over the hump. The instant he felt his tires grab a purchase he gunned it, but the Blazer slid anyway, its rear end swinging out toward the edge, slithering down that smooth, damp stone, and then for a second that would not end I saw a tire spinning over the emptiness, and then *bump, bump, skid* and he was across, skewed almost sideways in the narrow road directly in front of me.

"That one damn near went off in my hand," he said, incandescent.

The rest of the way was a long leveling out. The road widened comfortably, and we came at last to a gate—an official-looking bar, closed against our exit. For a minute I was afraid we would have to resort to destruction of government property, but the bar was not locked. We drove through the gate into the back-yard of a local college, right behind the cafeteria, crossed a stretch of lawn, and entered a campus road that delivered us onto the main drag of Young Harris, Georgia.

Billy noticed a gift shop and parked in front. Inside I found a lithograph of a trillium I thought Jane would like and recom-mended to Billy a book of poems by Bettie Sellers. The owner rang up our purchases and accompanied us to the door.

"Which way to Helen?" Billy asked.

"Which way did you come in?"

"Off the mountain," Billy said.

"The mountain?"

Billy pointed toward the imposing silhouette of Brasstown Bald looming above the little college across the street. "Brass-town."

"Godamighty," the man said. "In what?"

Billy was atop his own mountain now, enjoying the view. "That Blazer."

"I know for a fact," the man said, "that nobody's driven a vehicle down that road in three years. At least three years. Not one with more than two wheels. That road's been condemned."

Billy smiled. "Yeah."

I was feeling almost as exhilarated as if I had climbed my own mountain.

As we stepped onto the sidewalk, we heard the man call his wife from the back of the store. "Honey. Look here a minute."

HIGH BLOOD

JUST ABOVE the toilet, directly in front of my eyes, hangs a framed stanza of verse:

> There's a race of men that don't fit in,
> A race that won't sit still.
> They break the hearts of kith and kin
> And roam the world at will.

Singsong doggerel by Robert W. Service, but it nails Billy Claypoole like an epitaph, throws a little light on this guy John Trotter too, whose facilities I'm availing myself of. Billy has whisked me off to the ice and snow of the north Georgia mountains to meet him, the purpose of the trip no more defined than that, for grouse season's over and it's too cold to fish.

All I know about John Trotter is what I've heard from Billy, that he's a native of these mountains, an outdoorsman of no mean skill, and a bachelor. I suppose he subscribes to the sentiments of the Service verse, since he has hung it on the wall above the john.

I have no idea whether women ever use this bathroom, but it occurs to me that if they should, they would have nothing but blank wall to stare at. If they are in a hurry, they might miss the poetry altogether.

That's just as well, I suppose. From what I've seen of it, this house is a man's domain. One of the window frames in the den is decorated with a chain of turkey beards—just the sort

of thing most wives won't abide—and there was a bottle of
Jack Daniels sitting out on the kitchen table when we passed
through, though that may have been in celebration of our
coming and not part of the usual decor. If John belongs so tri-
umphantly to that race of men who break the hearts of kith
and kin by roaming the world as they please, he seems to be
too much of a gentleman to force a female guest to read about
it while she sits on the toilet.

I am here by my wife's permission, more or less freely
granted. Some of my friends envy me that freedom, some resent
it. "You wouldn't catch my wife letting me take off like you
do." Some say it with pride, as though they think they are lucky
to be married to such sensible women. Some are almost sanc-
timonious. They have outgrown such irresponsibilities; they
have gutters to clean. I have gutters too, but the ones that need
cleaning on a regular basis are inside my head. Most of the time
Jane understands.

A couple of John's friends have stopped by—game wardens
who have time for just one drink before getting on home to
their families. Billy is at the stove, sautéing shrimp he's brought
from the coast. The rest of us are sitting at the kitchen table—
formica top—John and the game wardens telling stories—true
stories mostly and well rehearsed. The subject is husbands. One
of the game wardens, for example, tells about a guy named
Norris—a cousin of his maybe—that was bad to chase women.
Came home one evening and found his wife gone, "and he ain't
left that doublewide since. Just sits there drinking beer and
watching wrassling on TV."

John says that if Norris had had sense enough to do that
from the start, he'd still have a wife.

The game warden says he went by to see Norris the other
day, says Norris had pulled his chair around to where he could

hit the back bedroom with his empty beer cans, says the room was beer cans wall to wall. "You aim to fill it all the way up before you start in on another'n?" the game warden asked.

Nah, said Norris, he just liked to have him something to stomp. When the room got to where you couldn't walk in it, he'd go in there and commence to stomping cans, stomp ever' goddam one of 'em, flatter'n a road-kill possum. Made him feel better. Made the cans weigh more too, for whenever he went to sell 'em.

The game warden asked him how he figured that.

"You stomp that hollow air out of 'em, they got to weigh more. It just makes sense."

"She didn't leave him for chasing women," John said. "Son-ofabitch's too damn dumb to live with. Terminal, I mean."

John and the game wardens grew up together right here. Their timing has been fine-tuned through years of practice. They could take their show on the road. One of them asks John if he's seen Cleveland lately.

"Last week," he says. "Saw him at the store."

For my benefit John explains that Cleveland is an old fellow who lives with his aged parents in a cove outside of town, comes in to buy groceries once a month.

"They doing all right?"

"Same as always. I said, 'Cleveland, how's Garfield and Frony?'

"'Ahh, they ain't doing no good, no good a-tall.' He's been saying that for fifteen years that I *know* of. Same thing ever' time: 'They just ain't doing no good a-tall.'"

II

After supper now. The game wardens are long gone, and John and Billy and I are riding around, negotiating snowy roads in

Billy's Cherokee. They are in the front seat, drinking beer. I'm in the back, trying to stay warm. A weird light reflected by the snow illumines the inside of the vehicle. I have no idea where we are, don't care.

"Let's head on up this cove," John says.

After a while Billy stops. A gate bars our way. In the head-lights a sign announces the entrance to a Wildlife Management Area. John directs our attention to a house on the right, a small dark box in a snowy field back off the road. One window is aglow.

"That's where Garfield and Frony live," John says. "Tap your horn."

The horn sounds too loud.

Directly, a porch light comes on. Then the door opens and a man steps out into the weak yellow glow. He's tall and stooped.

John lowers the window, yells, "Evening, Cleveland. This is John."

Cleveland says, "Evening, John."

"Just passing, Cleveland, wondered how y'all was get-ting on."

" 'Bout the same."

"Well, how's Garfield and Frony? They doing all right, are they?"

"Nahh, they ain't doing no good. No good a-tall. You'uns come on in now and speak to them."

"Y'all want to?" John asks, but he's already opening the door before Billy and I can say okay.

Cleveland receives us like a gentleman, holds the door as we stamp snow from our boots. A thermometer on the front wall says sixteen degrees.

The room we enter is shut off from the rest of the house. Hot, it smells strongly of cat. An old man and woman sit on either side of a wood-burning stove in quilt-draped chairs. The rest of the furniture includes a small table and two double beds, one of which is covered by a spread that bears the design of a pouch of Red Man chewing tobacco, the bright Indian head logo in the center. Except for that spot, the entire room—floor, walls, ceiling, stove, beds, old man and woman and the chairs in which they sit—is the color of snuff.

John greets them, introduces Billy and me as friends. Cleveland invites us to sit. We find spots on the beds. A cat appears at my feet, the same color as the room, crosses the floor, sits, and disappears into the background.

"Cleveland tells me y'all been slowing down some lately," John says to Frony.

Frony does not say a word, her mouth a sealed crease between her nose and her chin, but Garfield does. "She ain't no good no more. She's done got to where she'll not hardly get up out of that chair. Been down in her back, and she don't see like she used to. Me and him has to do for her a right smart now."

"I does for myself," Frony says, working her gums. "He can't cross this room without he has to get down on his knees like a young'un."

It strikes me that Garfield is molded to the shape of the chair.

"Rheumatiz' acts up sometimes," the old man explains. "Gives me a fit."

I spy another cat moving along the far wall.

Cleveland says he caught his daddy crawling across the yard the other day, just before it snowed. It was all he could do to get him back in the house.

"I known snow to stay on the ground forty-three days one year," Garfield says. "And hit come three good rains and didn't melt hit."

"What were you doing outside, Garfield," John asks, "cold as it is?"

Garfield's right hand strays toward a table, and a cat materializes at his touch. The cat stretches, arching its back against the old man's hand. Garfield kneads the cat like dough. "I had me something to do."

The walls of the room are decorated with an assortment of junk—antique rifles, license plates, obsolete funeral home calendars, a flaking metal sign advertising an extinct soda pop, magazine pictures of glamorous women—anything that will hang fairly flat.

John directs my attention to the rifles. "You know what those are?"

"That top one's kilt Yankees," Garfield says.

It's a muzzle loader, its cracked stock held together with baling wire.

"That's was my old grand-pap's gun. Hit come down from the war."

"I thought these mountain counties were Unionist," I venture.

"We'uns fit Yankees."

The way he says that gives me a little shiver, as though he believes that he himself bore arms in that conflict.

"Ain't seen a b'ar in eight years," Garfield says. "Last 'un I seen was a-crossing that field yonder, down by the crick. Seen him one evening about sundown, a-setting on the porch. Ain't seen ne'er a one since. Reckon what's come of them?"

"How old you think I am?" Cleveland asks John.

"I wouldn't have no idea, Cleveland. How old are you?"

Cleveland grins. "I ain't a-going to tell you." Then he gets up from the bed, reaches for a license plate hung high on the wall—a Georgia tag for a half-ton pickup, 1927—and hands it to John. It has been repainted, black numerals on a white background, by hand, with what looks like ordinary house paint.

"Is that the year you were born?" John asks.

Cleveland is smiling. "That it is."

"Then I'd guess you must be about sixty-one years old."

Cleveland's smile widens. "Now how'd you know that?"

"Is that right? Sixty-one?"

I can't tell who is fooling who, but Cleveland is embarrassed to show such pleasure. He tucks his head. "Yeah. Mama and Daddy's been married sixty-two years today."

"Oh," says John. "Is that right, Frony? Today's your wedding anniversary? Well, congratulations."

Billy and I join in.

Frony doesn't respond, but her eyes twinkle with amusement.

"Sixty-two years," says Garfield. "Hit takes a sight of living to live up sixty-two full years."

"And all of it right here?" Billy asks.

"Right in this here hollow. The old house burnt up. This un's new."

I have noticed two more cats, for a total now of five that I have seen moving at one time. There could be more.

John asks Garfield if he ever made liquor.

"Nosir, that's one thing I ain't ever done."

Frony begins to laugh. I would not know it if I were not looking at her, for it's a noiseless laughter at first, a tremor of breast and shoulders that works its way up to her chin, loosens her clamped jaws, exposing toothless gums, and issues forth at last in soft coughs.

"Sounds like Frony's telling on you, Garfield," John says.

Cleveland is rocking back and forth on his corner of the bed, thoroughly enjoying his father's plight, as eager as we are to hear the old man's answer.

"Well, I might have run a little, but hit were a long time

back," Garfield allows at last. "And never no more than what we needed for ourself."

"Did they ever bust up your still?"

"Lord God. Prettiest little copper still you ever saw one time. Taken a ax to it. And me a-standing there watching 'em do it."

"It would take a mean man to do that."

"Nah, he weren't mean. He was some of my ma's people, from over in Gilmer County. He made a good sheriff. Shore did. He'd let you go as long as he could, but ever' now and then he had to go out a-hunting stills to keep his job. Said he hated when he found one."

As we get up to leave, John asks the old couple if he can do anything for them. Frony says she don't need nothing except somebody to read to her out of the Bible; her eyes ain't no good no more. John does not volunteer for that service, but when Garfield says he'd fancy some more of that apple butter John brought him once, John says, "You got it."

Driving back to John's house, John explains that Cleveland is Garfield and Frony's only child. He doesn't know why they did not have more. Some people in town think that Cleveland is incapable of looking after the old people in their debilitated condition, he's getting on up in years himself. They should be put in some kind of nursing home where they could get decent care.

III

The next morning, blue sky and blinding glare, twenty-two degrees. We are climbing Springer Mountain toward the southern terminus of the Appalachian Trail, laboring through hip-deep drifts. Billy leads the way, breaking trail, as he should, since this is his idea. I'm bringing up the rear, behind John

Trotter, but still the going is tough. Soon my feet are wet and numb with cold, tripping over buried branches. After twenty minutes, I've dropped far behind, but I can see them through bare trees high above me. John has switched places with Billy. I'm impressed by their stamina, disheartened by my lack of it.

I don't know why I'm doing this. I have followed Billy through rougher conditions, but there were usually ducks or turkeys or grouse or trout at the end of those ordeals. All that awaits us at the top of Springer Mountain is the gateway to the Appalachian Trail. And a view, I guess.

That reminds me of a story, and suddenly things come together. Two years ago Billy invited a man named Jake to our hunting camp at Groton, a state trooper from one of these mountain counties who flew a helicopter in search of marijuana patches hidden in cornfields, and Jake told us about an old fellow who lived back up in the hills with his parents. One day Jake landed his helicopter in their yard and invited the man to take a ride with him. The man's face lit up. He turned to his mother, but she said, "Son, you know you got that high blood. You don't need to be a-going up in the air in nothing such as that."

When the man turned back to Jake, his face had collapsed, all folds and wrinkles like the face of a sad dog. "I got this high blood," the man said. "I don't need to be a-going up the air in nothing such as that."

"Aw hell," Jake said, "we won't go no higher than that there poplar tree, just to where you can see your place from the air."

The man looked back at his mother. She shook her head, and he reported the decision to Jake with a sad shake of his own.

"And him damn near sixty years old," Jake told us.

And that's who that was—Garfield and Frony, as molded to each other's contours after sixty years as they are to the chairs they sit in, and Cleveland the issue of that union, who cleaves not to a wife but remains forever a child, arrested in that first dependency.

I can no longer see John and Billy, but the trail they have broken in the snow ascends before me, higher and higher, switching back and forth through bare trees. All I have to do is follow it, one foot in front of the other. But how much farther? For all I know, they might be well on their way to Maine by now, unable to resist the open invitation to walk unimpeded clear to Mount Katahdin. Talk about high blood.

Several years ago I was asked to give a lecture on William Faulkner to a group of high school honors students who were being recruited by the University of Georgia. It was during July, oppressively hot, and for the first time that summer I put on a coat and tie. Jane was out of town for a few days—not an unusual circumstance—and I had given little thought to her absence. But as I walked toward the auditorium, I caught my reflection in a window, and suddenly it seemed to me that the dressed-up professor in the glass was someone else. I thought, *why am I doing this? Jane's not here.* On the face of it, that makes no sense, but the feeling shook me. I have wondered ever since if that momentary sensation was a symptom of a condition that goes by the ugly name *uxoriousness,* if I am so deeply married that I have no sense of myself apart from us as a couple. I see Cleveland's sad face repeating his mother's refusal to grant permission, but I shake it off: *Jane is your wife, man, not your mother.*

Mount Katahdin in any case is too damn far for me. But I'll make it to the top of Springer Mountain, just to where I can see my place from up in the air.

Part 2

TAKEN BY STORM

MY GRANDFATHER spent the last thirty years of his life in bed, victim of an assortment of chronic maladies. During my childhood, he seemed to suffer one crisis after another—the deliriums of high fever, internal bleeding, and once, a stroke that left him tangled in the sheets at the foot of the bed. These afflictions took him and us by storm. The news would come crackling through the long-distance wire, my mother's face revealing on the phone the danger he was in. I always had trouble accepting it. Since I had never seen him in such extremity, I could not imagine him without the authority of his faculties, and the thought of him caught helpless in the throes of fever confused and frightened me, as though he had been swept out on some dire passage from which he would not return. But return he would. By summer, when we went to visit them, Doc would have recovered, keen and full of wit, ready to resume his discourse on Shakespeare, fishing, baseball, and the Bible.

But that was as well as he got. I never saw him out of bed except when he was hobbling to the bathroom supported by my grandmother, and then I was shocked to see how small and weak his body was. When I was older, I asked my mother what was wrong with him. A lot of things, she said—allergies, digestive problems, migraine headaches; Doc had never been well. I could not understand why any of those conditions would make a complete invalid of a man, but apparently they had.

Instead of complaining, Doc laughed at his infirmities, often describing himself by quoting Shakespeare's Jaques: "second childishness and mere oblivion, sans teeth, sans eyes, sans taste, sans everything." An ordained minister, he wrote what he called sermonettes for a local paper. People came from all over the state to see him.

When Doc was in his mid-seventies, he and my grandmother (whom everyone knew as Buddie) moved to a house on a hydro-electric lake outside of town, bought a boat, and, to the extent permitted by health and weather, went fishing. They did it more for his sake than for hers. Among his passions fishing was the one he had continued to insist on, and through the years of his long decline she had cheerfully contrived ways to get him on the water. But they were too old now, their children thought, too old to go out on big water in a boat by themselves.

To a child that boat was a wonder. When we visited them in the summer, we would find it tied to the dock in front of the house, the July sun bouncing water shadows all along its dark green sides. In itself it was unremarkable, a twelve-foot skiff no different from a hundred similar craft on the lake. What made it noticeable to the neighbors and irresistibly enticing to us was the way my grandmother had converted it into a floating bed-room. With energy and resourcefulness, Buddie had equipped the boat with a folding cot and a blue and yellow beach um-brella that stood in a socket bolted to the floor. The neighbors soon grew accustomed to the sight of the old couple working up and down the shoreline. When the umbrella was open, one said, they looked like the owl and the pussycat.

The news of Doc's adventure came long-distance from Buddie one morning in July. In its first telling it was not so much a story as a series of exclamations—self-reproach, exaspera-tion, and relief. Later, as my mother and her sister compared versions, they pieced together a coherent narrative. It began with my aunt's calling Buddie from her home in Columbia and asking her to drive down for the day. Doc had been free of serious illness the whole spring and into the summer. So Buddie put aside her customary reservations about leaving him and arranged for Liza, a kind and gentle black woman, to stay until she got back that night.

Liza had served my grandparents as maid, cook, and nurse off and on for more than thirty years. Almost as old as Doc and no longer in good health herself, she came now only once a week, often on Saturday so she could sit with Doc and listen to the baseball game—they were both Brooklyn Dodger fans. I had heard my mother and her sister laughing about that arrangement. "I can't imagine what Liza could do if Daddy really needed help," my mother said. "Other than call the ambulance."

The morning Buddie left for Columbia, Liza told her not to worry. Just go on and have a good time, she said, we'll be just fine.

"Just don't let him talk you into going fishing," Buddie said. "I don't want to have to worry about him all the way to Columbia and back."

Liza laughed. "I might could get him down there, but how us gonna get back up? That's what I want to know. I wouldn't be no more help to him than he would to me. And wouldn't that be a fix. You go on now. We be just fine."

From his bed Doc could see the water. He held out until early afternoon.

I can imagine Liza's attempts to dissuade him and just as easily his persistence. They were such good friends it must have been a gentle tug of war.

"And where you gonna sit? Tell me that."

"Why, I'll lie on my cot, Liza."

"Oh no you ain't. Not in that boat you ain't. Miz Lawton done said not to let you go fishing in the first place. I sho ain't gonna help you climb in no boat."

"I'll be perfectly all right, Liza. The boat is tied to the dock. It's not going anywhere."

"Why can't you lay in that long folding chair she got? I'll put that out for you and you can fish right there from the dock."

"I just like the feel of water beneath me."

With Doc behind her, gripping her frail shoulders, Liza led him down to the lake. They went even more slowly than usual because of an angry ingrown nail on his big toe. She murmured her disapproval all the way. Easing him into the boat was tricky, but they managed. She even got the umbrella up, though that turned out to be wasted effort, for soon after he was settled a dark cloud covered the sun.

While he fished, she sat on the dock and shelled butter beans. For a while they argued about who should make the All-Star team. Then Doc complained about the failure of the fish to bite and Liza worried about the cloud. Finally, she got to her feet. "We better be getting back up to the house now. It look like it fixing to bust loose any minute."

"We sure do need it all right, but you know as well as I do that it's been clouding up like this every afternoon for two weeks and we haven't had a good shower yet." When she didn't respond, Doc added, "What I really want to do is go down yonder to that little cove."

"Well, you just gonna have to want to 'cause drive that boat is one thing I can't do."

"What I was thinking is that you could take the rope and pull me along the bank. It's not very far. Do you think you could do that?"

Liza untied the rope and stepped carefully from the dock to the ground. Then with the skiff in tow she picked her way along the rocky red-clay beach just above the waterline. The boat followed easily. They were about halfway to the cove when the wind hit. A stiff breeze at first, it filled the umbrella like a sail. The rope stretched taut. Liza tried to hold the boat, but it pulled her into the shallows. She set her heels in the soft bottom, but a gust hit her from behind and struck the side of the boat like a big fist. She pitched forward. Reaching to catch herself, she let go of the rope. Doc yelled to her, but the wind was roaring in her ears. By the time she got to her feet and back on the bank, the boat was too far out for shouting, but she hollered anyway, "Hold on!" and waved her arms.

Since Doc never gave his version of the event, the story always abandoned him at this point and followed Liza back to the house, where she called everybody she could think of. But each time I heard it I stayed beside the lake, wondering how Doc managed to ride out the storm. He never said. Maybe he was too embarrassed to talk about it. But I have lived long enough now to have learned something about boats in a storm. With a surer sense of my own mortality, I find it easy to imagine that I am out there on the water with my grandfather.

Doc's first concern was Liza. His eyes were too weak to make out her features, but he could feel her distress in the way she rocked and waved. He wanted to comfort her, assure her that it was all his fault; but there was no time to fret about that. The umbrella was fluttering loudly. Bellied against the wind, it threatened to pull loose the board through which it was bolted and tear a hole in the plywood floor. Maybe he could lift it from its socket. But just as he was reaching for it, the ribs broke with a loud pop, and the blue and yellow canvas folded into a huge shriveled flower.

Instantly, he could feel the difference in the motion of the boat, but he was well offshore by then, too far out to consider paddling, even if he had had the strength. The motor was his only hope, but even Buddie sometimes had trouble getting it started; he doubted he could pull the rope hard enough. Easing his way from the cot to the seat in the stern, he noticed Liza, still on the bank. He waved her on toward the house. She waved back. He tilted the motor into the water and gave the cord a pull. No use. Liza was toiling up the hill, into the wind. He lay back against the corner of the stern, exhausted, and urged her on.

Liza made it to the house and disappeared inside. Help should be coming soon. He wondered if the sheriff had a boat.

But maybe he wouldn't need the sheriff. When he turned, he saw a spit of land ahead, a bare red-clay point that reached like a tongue into the lake. It was still some distance off. For a few minutes he dared to believe he might run aground on it. Closer, he reached for the paddle at his feet and tried to rudder the boat to the left, but, shoved by the gusts, the vessel kept no steady course. Heeling first one way and then another, it missed the point by fifty feet. He could see the bottom as he crossed the underwater bar.

In the heavy chop of open water, the boat began to pitch and roll. Whitecaps broke against the bow, spraying his face. He grasped the handle of the motor for balance and support. And felt a surge of exhilaration. He was on his own. At first he did not know whether the thrill he felt was that of joy or fear. Total dependence had become such a habit his mind was slow to realize that for the first time in thirty years he was free of the well-meaning solicitude of wife and children, the orders of doctors and nurses, the confining bed. He was beginning to enjoy this. Then he remembered: This was the way it used to feel to get up from bed after a long bout with malaria and drive an automobile again, or to enter the woods with a gun, or to decide when and where he was going fishing and for how long. Like a child behind the steering wheel, he gripped the handle harder and pretended he was really in control of speed and direction.

But his body was not up to the game. Accustomed to being on his back, he soon needed something to lean against, and, because he was lightly dressed, he wanted protection from the wind and spray. The bow of the boat was decked with plywood. The area beneath it was small, but if he could get to the front, he would fit. He would have to manage on his own, of course—a tricky business with the boat rolling in the swell—and he would have to do it now, while he still had control of his arms and legs. Already his feet were growing numb from the slosh of water in the bottom, and he was beginning to shiver.

He looked toward the shore, but his glasses were fogged and without them he could not distinguish between land and lake. He had no idea where he was, but he knew that rescue was unlikely now. This was the kind of storm forecasts warned about. He had heard their bulletins on the radio: Small craft advised to stay off of area lakes. Maybe he was closer to the other side than he knew. In any case, he had to get to the front of the boat if he expected to be alive when he landed.

He took it slowly, stern to cot, cot to bow, more like an inchworm than a man, he thought. In the process he struck his bad toe against something hard, and for a moment he thought he might vomit, but the throbbing soon subsided to an ache he could stand. Holding on to the bent shaft of the umbrella, he lowered himself to the floor and crawled forward into the shelter. He found life jackets there and put one on. It pillowed him against the sides and provided a little warmth. Except for the pitching of the boat, which in that position made him dizzy, he might have been almost comfortable.

His toe no longer hurt. He knew why. He reached for his foot but grasped his knee and remembered the death of Falstaff. "Then I felt to his knees," the hostess said, "and so upward and upward, and all was as cold as any stone." If death came now in the wind and rain—for it had begun to rain—he would be glad at least not to die like Falstaff, in a strange bed, babbling of green fields. That was the fear he had lived with all these years—not death, but dying in a hospital, attended by strangers. He was surprised to feel so drowsy, to think that he might actually be able to sleep in such a wet, wildly rocking bed. Jesus had. He knew that. In the storm on the Sea of Galilee. Until his frightened friends woke him with the question, Carest thou not that we perish?

What woke Doc was the jolt and then the grating of rocks against the underside of the boat. He lay still for a long time. Now and then a small wave lifted the stern. He began to realize he was landed. He opened his eyes and concluded that the rain had stopped. After a while he looked for something to grab hold of, found it, and dragged himself from his nest in the bow. Now he could reach the gunwale and pull himself up to a kneeling position. He didn't know what had happened to his glasses. He felt around on the floor and then gave up. What he saw when he looked resembled a house, white and perched on a hill above the water. If the people were at home, they should be coming down to get him. Maybe it was a vacation house, unoccupied this week. He would have to get out of the boat and see for himself.

It took him almost an hour to crawl across the slick, rocky beach and up the grassy hill. Several times he had to stop and rest. By the time he made it, knees bruised and bad toe throbbing again, he knew the house was empty. So he turned and leaned back against a banister and looked out upon the lake. The calm water reflected rosy clouds and illumined the air between lake and sky. As the sun went down, the colors faded. Doc drew in his legs against the chill and waited to be found.

"They found him under the steps of a house across the lake," the story always ended. "Right at dark. Somebody spotted the boat, I guess, and followed his tracks." They had him back in his own bed safe and sound by the time Buddie got home that night.

What my grandparents said to each other never got into the story. It may not have been much. What good after all would scolding have done when Doc was already back in his bed, propped on his pillow? And how could he have explained to her that having passed through the storm to the glow of a still place he felt a little better prepared for the next time?

OPEN HOUSE

FOR the last two weeks a summer tanager has been pecking at the window in our den. All day he's at it, fluttering, breast to glass, peck, peck, peck. I know, of course, what he's doing. He is mistaking his reflection for a rival tanager. Cardinals and mockingbirds are famous for the same behavior, but I have not known either of those species to sustain its belligerence for so long.

At first I was glad to have the tanager. Wild creatures have always been welcome in our yard. My wife and I put out nest boxes for titmice, crested flycatchers, wood ducks, and screech owls; we keep the feeders filled with sunflower seeds and the birdbath with clean water. I let the grass grow high around the edges of the yard for rabbits, and chipmunks entertain us on the stone wall outside our den. So I was pleased when I noticed that summer tanagers were building on an oak limb within view of our breakfast table. In past years I had heard them calling from the woods below the house, but they had never nested in the yard. And they are beautiful. In contrast to the subdued plumage of most songbirds, theirs is glamorous—the male totally bright red, the female just as completely yellow-green. Now that they had taken up residence on the oak limb, I was looking forward to seeing a lot of them. Little did I know.

When the male discovered the intruder in the window, I pulled up a chair. Indifferent to my presence or blinded by the reflection, the bird would launch forth from a stem of ivy that grew alongside, hit the window, and strike with his beak. For the second or two that he was splayed against the glass, light from behind shone through his wings and the spread feathers of his tail. I was glad for the opportunity to observe such a bird at close range, but as it became apparent that he meant to fight to the death, I began to worry that he might be the one to die, that, exhausted, he would flutter to the ground where the cats could get him. Instead, he always retreated to the ivy and after a moment's respite hurled himself again into the fray. I worried about the damage he might be doing to his beak. He was not a woodpecker. Nature had not equipped his kind to peck on glass all day, day after day. I could imagine how sore that beak must be getting. Dribbles of fluid soon flecked his corner of the window. But whether his beak was sore or not, I was getting tired of its constant tattoo. I cut out a silhouette of a hawk and taped it to the glass, but that had no effect at all. Next I covered the window with sheets of newspaper—no small task; it's a big window—but I succeeded only in blocking out the light. The obsessed tanager searched for his enemy up and down the narrow alleys of exposed glass, and, finding him at last, renewed his efforts to drive him from the yard.

The female, meanwhile, quietly kept the house. By looking closely I could see her on the nest, her beak motionless among the dappled leaves. When the eggs hatch out, I thought, the instinct to provide food for the babies will override her mate's mindless determination to defend his territory, and we'll all be relieved.

One day about this time I spotted a commotion on the oak limb. The male, of course, was too busy battering the window to notice the trouble at home, but I looked just in time to see a cowbird at the nest.

Cowbirds are the parasites of the avian world. Having missed out somehow on the nesting instinct, the female finds the active nest of another passerine species, and, while the parents are away, she deposits among the host clutch her own fertilized egg. The parents, none the wiser, incubate the alien along with their own, and when the eggs hatch, the baby cowbird, which is usually larger than his stepbrothers and -sisters, gets most of the food, often to the detriment of the legitimate occupants. The size of the cowbird flocks I see in the winter is an impressive sign of their success at this business, but I had never caught one in the act. Now I had, and so had the female tanager. With trumpets blaring *charge,* she swooped in on the interloper and drove her away. Anthropomorphically, I cheered, while her valiant mate, oblivious to her cries of alarm, continued to beat himself silly upon his own reflection. The only way to stop him now, I figured, would be to break the mirror he was using.

That, of course, was out of the question. Though he wasn't trying to get in, he looked like he was, and the window was there to keep things out.

At Walden Pond, Henry Thoreau flung open his door and windows to admit not only light and wind but birds and squirrels as well. Wanting to live intimately with nature, he refused even to begrudge wasps a warm place for the night.

The notion is appealing. Even as I enjoy the comforts of air-conditioning, I grumble about the artificial habitat it creates and fear that it may be costing me more than the hundred and fifty dollars I pay to the power company each month. Surely we could learn to tolerate a wider range of weathers than the narrow comfort zone marked on the thermostat. Then perhaps we might grow gradually more resistant to pollen and other irritants, impervious to mosquitoes, more sensitive to smells.

But the summer tanager, still pecking away at the window, forces me to admit that I'm not as hospitable as Thoreau. It also reminds me of a hornet that built a nest against our window screen several years ago.

Sitting in my living room one afternoon in May, I noticed

that one of the panes looked flyspecked. Closer, I saw that the dirtiness was on the screen—disparate flecks of matter clogging the little square holes. Even as I watched, the insect alighted, selected a space, and deposited into it a mouthful of some kind of broth. Whatever it was, hornet or wasp, the creature was boldly marked, white on black, reminding me of an outrageously patterned World War I fighter plane, a Fokker, say, designed to terrify. Its most menacing feature was its all-white face, as baleful as a skull. *Of course,* I thought, *a bald-faced hornet. But aren't they the ones that build those big nests, those heavy globes that hang in the summer woods? What is this one doing on my window screen?*

I called an entomologist I knew.

"Sounds like she's building a nest all right," he said. "But it's really unusual for that species to build against a vertical surface, especially up against a house. We had some captive insects in a lab once that built against the glass wall of the cage, but I don't think I've ever heard of that kind of thing in the wild."

"I've only seen one hornet," I said. "It must take more than one to build an entire nest."

"That's the queen. Among the Vespinae she's the only one that overwinters. About this time of year she comes out from behind the bark or wherever she's been for the last six months and begins to look for a nest site. She'll get it started, but as soon as the first workers hatch out, they'll take over and leave her free to lay eggs."

"So she's already fertilized?"

"Oh yeah. That happened last fall, before the males died. Frankly, I'd be surprised if she completes the nest in a place like that, but if she does, let me know. I'd like to come out and take a look. It would be a great opportunity to observe interior activity."

I always had an irrational fear of insects that fly and sting—

the kind of fear some people have of snakes—and I have been a relentless enemy, blasting their nests with Hotshot when I found yellow jackets excavating in the yard or wasps building under the eaves. But this was different. This was an opportunity, as my friend was saying, to observe the hornet's hidden life. I was reminded of the ant colonies I had imprisoned in mason jars when I was a child and how I had watched as they pursued their busy errands along exposed sections of tunnel. But the hornet's nest was better, the activity inside more complicated. From the comfort of my living room, protected by the glass, I would be able to observe their behavior as carefully as a scientist.

"If she does complete it," the entomologist continued, "you're going to have to be careful. Those nests get big in a hurry, and once the new queens start hatching out, the whole colony becomes protective. Along about August they get real mean, especially on days when the barometric pressure falls."

I felt a bit of a chill when he said that, but August was too far away to worry about, so I put a pad and pencil on the table by the window and settled in to watch the progress of the nest.

Typically, *Dolichovespula maculata* suspends its nest from a tree limb, beginning the operation by constructing along the underside a thin sheet that tapers into a triangle. At the bottom the hornet elongates the point into a petiole, and upon that she fashions the first cluster of cells. My hornet, however, continued to clog the holes of the screen with wet paper. After three days, the random flecks assumed a pattern, something like a horseshoe about three inches across, apparently the base against which the nest would be constructed. When I looked again, the hornet had fashioned an eave that extended from the top of the horseshoe, and against the underside of that she went to work on an appendage that turned soon into a cluster of hexagonal cylinders. The comb comprised no more than six or eight of these cells. As the hornet worked on it, the whole structure moved a little from side to side like a bell.

The eave and comb took the hornet more than a week to complete, so I expected the housing, the outer shell that entomologists call the envelope, to take at least that long. Instead, she managed it in just a day or two. When I returned from work one afternoon, there it was, the finished product, small but complete. From the outside it resembled a hemispheric cone, a gray, papery whelk, clamped against the window screen. At the bottom it tapered into a tube, and at the end of the tube was an opening. Even as I watched, the hornet came crawling out and flew away.

Back inside, with a flashlight fixed upon the interior of the nest, I awaited the return of the queen. That did not take long. Suddenly she was at the lip of the tube, and in a moment she was emerging from its hole into the chamber, where she resumed her work upon the comb. I could not see closely enough to tell whether she was building new cells, laying eggs, or feeding larvae, but whatever the task she did it with purpose and deliberation, crawling back and forth across the open ends of the cells, flexing her abdomen upon them, tending them with her legs. Only at night did she rest.

For several days I noticed no further development of the nest, no increase in its size, inside or out, but one day two new hornets appeared, smaller insects and darker than the queen. I turned on the flashlight and saw inside a third, still wet and folded, just emerged from its cell. It crawled down into the tube and a moment later appeared at the lip. There it waited for several minutes, until, dried by light and air, it opened its wings and zoomed away.

By the end of the next day I was able to count four workers. These insects, whose genetic codes prepared them for work on a free-hanging globe, began their labor by increasing the area of the base, daubing the holes of the screen with a mash of chewed wood. Next they papered over the outer shell, layer by layer, until raised latitudinal bands appeared. They were of the subtlest woody pastels—pale gray-green, mauve, faint lavender—colors bearing witness to the kinds of wood chosen by the hornets.

As the outer shell expanded, the size of the chamber increased proportionately, making room for the growing comb. That was the queen's sole business now. Freed from the task of constructing the hive, she devoted herself to the nursery with maternal solicitude, fondling the comb, tamping it, turning it this way and that.

As the days lengthened toward the solstice, the queen became more fervent, and I spent longer stretches at the window. For the first time in years I was ignoring the return of summer birds. Waves of warblers moved through the treetops without my going outside to watch; the songs of wood thrushes came floating up in the late afternoons from the woods below my house, and still I kept my vigil at the window. From time to time I heard the staccato calls of summer tanagers but hardly paused even to wonder where they were nesting. My fascination with the hornets had grown as fervent as the labor of the queen.

"How much longer are you going to let it go on?" my wife asked one day.

"I don't know."

"If you wait much longer, and I really don't see how you can, it could be a real problem to get rid of."

That was truer than she realized but not in the way she meant. By some genetic glitch, I surmise, this queen had built a nest in such a way and such a place that the tender life inside was vulnerable not only to my eye but to a blast of insecticide as well, sprayed through the screen. Apparently indifferent to her unprotected rear, the queen felt secure behind the barrier of tough paper she and her offspring had constructed. Like my own house, hers braved the outside world, the pestiferous environment that always threatens. Hornets or not, I couldn't bring myself to take that kind of advantage of her mistake.

"You're not thinking about letting it go on all summer, are you?"

"Maybe we could put a sign out front," I said. "'DANGER: HORNETS AT WORK—USE BACK DOOR.' Hand-lettered in red."

My wife did not answer.

By June 22 the nest was as big as a man's fist, sculpted and smooth. The tube had disappeared, and, on the inside, the workers had begun a second tier of cells. From first light to dark, hornets came and went, bringing food to their little larval sisters. By flashlight I could see what appeared to be an interaction between workers and pupae that I took to be feeding. Other workers continued to enlarge the nest, and the queen kept on laying eggs.

One day when the colony had increased to perhaps twelve or fifteen workers, I opened the window. With nothing but screen between the nest and me, I detected an odor, faint but distinctive, a kind of dry organic smell. As I drew nearer, the insects inside began to buzz. Suddenly, the screen seemed a flimsy barrier, and I was reminded of a story I had heard from a friend named Joe. When he was in high school, he and a buddy, riding around in the woods in a four-wheel drive, bumped into a hornet's nest, bashed it with the windshield. They just had time to get the windows up. Though they were protected by the glass, Joe said, the fury of the hornets' attack was unnerving. Before long, the windshield was wet with toxin, but it was the high-pitched hum of the hornets' rage that really undid them. Joe's friend wet his pants. I closed the window on the nest, and firmly resolved to stop this business before August. As things turned out, I was spared that disagreeable task.

A day or two later, just past first light, my wife awakened me with an urgent call: "Come quick," she said. "Something's happening to the hornets!"

I stumbled into the living room, trying to bring the world into focus, and knelt at the window. Rubbing sleep from my eyes, I was confronted by a summer tanager—a red flurry in the dim light, inches from my face, beating the air. The bird was darting at the nest, attacking with its heavy beak—swoop, flutter, and strike—breaking ragged holes in the tough paper shell. I flinched. From where I knelt, daylight opened in the envelope. The comb was exposed. I saw larvae extending from their cells like blind fingers, and the tanager was picking them, one by one. *Where are the workers?* I wondered. *Why aren't they protecting the nest? And where is the queen?* The yellow-green female joined her mate; he flew up onto a branch for a moment but soon returned and completed the pillage. It was all over in a minute or two.

I went outside. The nest was utterly ravaged. Tatters of paper clung to the screen. The comb of cells, so long in construction, was broken off and lay on the ground below, empty of occupants. From the oak above I heard the static calls of the tanagers, *p-tek-a-tek, p-tek-a-tek.*

The tanagers that nested outside the window this year are gone. I never saw the brood hatch out, though I watched. About the time they were due, we had a week of rain. When the skies cleared, the nest was abandoned. Maybe the cool wet weather, the incessant rain and wind, chilled the nestlings even as they were hatching, or it could have been a cowbird, starving out its smaller foster siblings, but I don't think so. I want to believe they all survived, the whole family skulking off into the dripping overstory when no one was looking. In any case, the male left behind a window fouled by specks of hardened fluid—little apostrophes of bird spit, I guess—as strong a reminder as the remains of the hornet nest, which still clogs my screen, of our losing battle against things that want in.

A GIFT FROM THE BEAR

IT'S A RARE THING these days to come face to face with a wild animal that is powerful enough to kill you. In the lower forty-eight your best bet is Glacier or Yellowstone National Park. It's not likely even in those places, but it is possible because grizzlies live there. I say not likely. Thousands of campers and fishermen hike the backcountry trails every summer without finding so much as a pile of dry bear scat. Yet my friend Billy Claypoole saw a grizzly on his first trip to Yellowstone. With a man from Bozeman, Montana, he was riding horseback on a trail above the Yellowstone River. Crossing a sagebrush flat, Billy happened to turn in the saddle and look back to the left—he told me later that something made him turn—and there on a lower terrace stood the bear, upright like a man, its long hair rippling silver in the wind and sun, watching them. Billy spoke softly to his friend, who was riding up ahead. The man turned and saw. "Don't stop," he said.

Paul Schullery, who writes as well about Yellowstone as anyone I've read, says that's the way to see your griz, "a chance meeting on his doorstep."

I asked Billy how close he was to the bear.

"A hundred yards," he said. "Maybe less."

I sort of wish I had been with them that day. I would like to know how it feels to be that close to an uncaged grizzly, how the skin must suddenly become fully conscious of its own delicacy, the bones of their fragility, the mind of its precarious equilibrium. There may be virtue in that kind of knowing. Barry Lopez in *Arctic Dreams* explains what might have happened when a young Eskimo, alone on the ice and armed only with primitive weapons, faced a polar bear. "To encounter the bear, to meet it with your whole life, was to grapple with something personal. The confrontation occurred on a serene, deadly, and elevated plain. If you were successful you found something irreducible within yourself, like a seed. To walk away was to be alive, utterly. To be assured of your own life, the life of your kind. . . . It was to touch the bear. It was a gift from the bear."

Of course, you might not walk away. Like all bears, grizzlies are unpredictable, and they can kill an elk with one blow to the neck. To realize the power that takes, Schullery suggests, "ask yourself how long you'd have to hit an elk with your hand to kill it." I don't want to contribute to the grizzly's undeserved reputation as a slavering, red-eyed beast that stalks campgrounds at night, but I had read too many accounts of maulings and fatalities to go out looking for a bear on the chance of receiving a gift from it.

Our son John on the other hand might not be so cautious. He was working at Yellowstone the summer Billy saw the bear. It was his fourth trip to the park and he was still looking for his first one. He would be outdone when I told him about Billy's luck.

I

I had spent my first night in Yellowstone eight years before, in a tent, wide awake with anxiety. My wife Jane lay next to me, sleeping soundly, and in the tent next door John and his two younger sisters snuggled together like puppies. Our site was on the back side of Pebble Creek Campground, closest to wilderness. Fifty yards behind us the creek babbled out of a narrow little gorge. I had read that a grizzly's nose can detect the smell of fried fish from two miles away. Though we had put our food in the trunk of the car and cleaned up our site, the campground was full. Among all those people you could bet that somebody had left food out. Somewhere above us a bear might be crossing the creek, nonchalant in the rushing current. I could see it pause, swing its heavy, shaggy head, nostrils flared to catch again that filament of scent, then turn and start downstream, not in a hurry but certain, emerging at last from the mouth of the gorge. Ours would be the first tents he came to. The smell of fried cutthroat trout lingered in my beard. I lay awake wishing I had washed it.

Of the one and a half million people who had visited Yellowstone Park during the seventies, only one had been killed by a bear. I had not read that statistic as I lay in my tent that night, but I did know that in the hundred years of the park's existence bears had killed no more than three people. I kept telling myself that there was a greater statistical probability of our being struck by lightning on this trip, a far greater chance of our dying in a car wreck on the drive back to Georgia.

But in that dark tent on the back side of Pebble Creek Campground statistics could not compete with my overheated imagination. For I had read graphic accounts in outdoor magazines of that dreadful night in the summer of '67 when grizzlies killed two young women in separate areas of Glacier Park. The one I couldn't forget was the attack on a group of college-age park employees camping by a lake. The bear came while they were sleeping, nosed among the sleeping bags, woke them up. The scene played before my eyes in living color—sudden cries of terror, cries of warning, confused scrambling in the dark, campers scampering up trees like squirrels, the coughing growls of the bear. One of the girls could not get out of her sleeping bag. The zipper stuck, or something. The report of her last words horrified the country, horrified me: "He's got my arm off. Oh God I'm dead."

In spite of the chill I unzipped my bag about halfway. Yet it was not my safety for which I was concerned as much as that of my wife and children. It occurred to me, half seriously, to sit outside the tents for the rest of the night, facing up Pebble Creek into the dark backcountry.

John awakened me in the early light with an urgent whisper, "Daddy, a moose!" I scurried out, pulling up my trousers. In the cold mist a mature bull, taller than the tallest tents, was loping through the sleeping campground. When it was gone, John and I agreed that we would rather have seen the moose in a backcountry beaver pond, but the mist helped—a gauze screen between us and the animal that all but obliterated context and flattened the creature into a black apparition.

My children laugh at me for fretting about their safety. I suppose they have reason, but at my age, I tell them, I have a better sense of the dangers; I know what can happen. I'm also bedeviled by an active imagination. Late in the afternoon of that same day, it was beginning to stir. John had gone fishing three hours before to Soda Butte Creek, no more than a six- or eight-minute walk from the highway across a wide meadow. From the campground you could see fishermen along its banks, small in the distance, casting. There was no reason to worry. "Just be sure you get back before dark," I had told him. "Well before dark."

In that northern latitude daylight lingers until after nine o'clock, but the sun had dropped by seven behind the wall of the creek gorge, throwing a shadow over our site. I had built a small fire, for warmth and cheer, and we were all waiting for John to get back so I could fry the fish we'd caught that morning and the ones I hoped he'd be bringing in from this trip.

At thirteen he was an experienced woodsman. I had been taking him duck hunting since he was big enough to wade into a beaver pond before daylight. The year before he had killed his first buck, alone in the woods, and dragged it out to the road; and with his scout troop he had survived harsh, cold-weather camping in a north Georgia mountain wilderness. I was only a little concerned that he wasn't back yet, but I figured I might as well walk out to the creek, meet him coming in. Eleven-year-old Sarah Jane wanted to go too.

At one point along the gravel road that led to the highway I showed Sarah Jane where two mule deer had crossed in front of John and me on our way to the stream that morning. They had surprised us, coming out of the trees on our right—two bucks, one a forkhorn, the other a big heavy-antlered deer. We had stopped and watched as they crossed Pebble Creek on our left and fed out across the sagebrush. We had been close enough to see the velvet of their racks.

If Sarah Jane and I didn't meet John on the road, I knew where to look. Fishing together that morning, we had discovered a pool where cutthroat were rising. He quickly caught two fish on his spinning rod, but, unable to release them from the treble hook without killing them, he asked to try my flyrod. I hesitated, afraid that the timing and that great length of line would be more than he could handle, but after some initial frustration he made a decent cast; the little humpy floated across a patch of light bedrock, and I saw the fish rise in the clear amber water. John set the hook, lifted the rod instinctively, and played the fish well, letting it run downstream before bringing it up against the current. It was a good cutthroat, maybe thirteen inches long. We admired its speckled dark golden back and on the underside of its gills the twin vermilion slashes from which it gets its name.

I was sure Sarah Jane and I would find him at the pool. Yet by the time we came in sight of it I knew somehow that John would not be there. I continued downhill anyway. Maybe I'd find his tracks in the gravel bar along the edge. When I found no sign of his having been there at all, I started upstream. Tall forest stood now on either side of the stream, climbing steeper hills, closing in, and it was darker along the floor of the narrow valley. At last we came to the mouth of Icebox Canyon. Beyond this point the sides were sheer rock walls. We could go no farther.

A sign board stood before us, marking the head of a trail that crossed the stream just below the mouth of the gorge. In the gathering dark I noticed a sign in Day-Glo orange; it bore the silhouette image of a bear and screamed: DANGER: GRIZZLY FREQUENTING AREA TRAVERSED BY THIS TRAIL. Good Lord. And my son was wandering around with a flyrod in his hand. I needed a ranger.

Sarah Jane and I hurried back down the highway.

"I bet he'll be there when we get back," she insisted.

I tried to calm my voice. "I bet so too."

We took a shortcut through the sagebrush flat that lay adjacent to the campground. Halfway across we came upon a figure standing before us in the dark, awaiting our approach. He was holding a flyrod in his hand. It was John.

"Where in the hell have you been?"

"Sir?" He seemed puzzled by my tone.

"We've been looking everywhere for you. Couldn't you tell it was getting dark?"

"It didn't seem that late."

I eased up. "You must have been catching fish."

"I didn't fish that long. They weren't biting."

"Then where have you been?"

He turned and pointed with the rod to the east. "Up there." I discerned the faint glimmer of what must have been a high meadow buttressing the rock wall of mountain. I knew an explanation was coming so I didn't trouble him with another question.

"You know those two mule deer we saw this morning?"

I did.

"Well, I was coming back along that little creek over there and I saw them."

"And you followed them."

"Yessir."

"Okay. Tell me about it."

John's account was so crosshatched with details of movement, distance, and terrain that I had trouble following it. What it amounted to was that he had managed to get downwind of the deer and hide behind a boulder.

"They came right by me. I could have touched the big buck."

Sarah Jane had gone on into camp, so Jane was aware of the stalk when we got there. But she and the girls were more interested in my frying trout than they were in the details of the hunt. I dipped each of the fish in a pan of milk, dusted it in flour, and dropped it into a skillet of hot oil. We ate in the light of a lantern. After a while, I asked John how it had felt to be out on that mountainside, alone, with dark coming on. And then those deer.

"It was a lot lighter up there than it was down here," he said.

"I guess it would have been."

"I don't know if I was close enough to actually touch the big buck, but if I had had a bow, I could have gotten him."

"That counts," I said. "The Plains Indians called it counting coup."

II

The summer after his junior year in college, John got a job with the park concessionaire busing tables at a lodge at Tower Junction. On the tenth of June came a postcard showing a Yellowstone griz. "No need for an explanation of what's on the front," he wrote. "I haven't seen one yet. I opened my fishing season last night at the Blacktail Lakes on the road to Mammoth where I'd heard coyotes howling the night before. On my third cast with a hare's ear I hooked a 13″ brook trout. (My first time using a wet fly.) The fish book by Paul Schullery says they rarely reach that size. But there's no doubt what it was. It was beautiful. Its belly was brilliant orange-red and the fins were edged with white. The speckles with the red on blue were nice too. Love, John." Two weeks later he reported that the stone-fly hatch was moving up the Yellowstone. Fishing would soon be great on the Lamar, Slough Creek, and Soda Butte. He begged us to come. And hurry, he said. The park was on fire.

Indeed it was. Because of drought and years of rigorous fire control that had left the park a tinderbox of deadfall and debris, lightning strikes and a campfire or two set half a million acres ablaze. By the time Jane and I drove out in early August, the fires were out of control. We entered through the northeast gate at dark, just a few miles above our old Pebble Creek Campground. From there down to Tower Junction thick blue smoke lay along the floor of the Lamar Valley. Across the river to the south a ragged ring of fire was eating a sore in the face of a mountain. From time to time we had to slow down for bison.

Heads lowered, the beasts stood in the smoky headlights, too miserable to yield right of way.

John crammed as much activity as possible into the week we were there. Toward the end, when my shoulders were sore and my legs dead from backpacking, he suggested Slough Creek.

On our way to Yellowstone seven years before, we had spent the night with a friend in Laramie who recommended that I fish Slough Creek. "The upper meadow's a must," he said. "Twenty-inch fish and easy to catch." Well, I had hoped. But a family vacation doesn't allow much opportunity for serious backcountry fishing. Since then the upper meadow of Slough Creek had been my favorite fishing fantasy. Now, John said, we could go. He had saved the best for last. To his surprise and consternation I hesitated. The thought of putting my blistered feet into heavy boots again was intolerable.

It was an awkward moment. At considerable inconvenience John had rearranged his work schedule to give me a full week of fishing. And here I was acting like an old man. It was not that I was out of shape, I reminded him, just unaccustomed to a thirty-pound pack and the altitude. He understood; didn't want to insist, but this would be my only chance to fish Slough Creek.

"How long a walk are we talking about?"

"Depends. If you want to fish the upper meadow, it's eight miles. The fishing's great but we'd have to camp."

"What's the middle section like?"

"Pretty heavily fished. It's not but two miles from the parking area. But we could do that if you want to."

From the trailhead we climbed through a steep forest of lodgepole pine. Dry woods. The soil as gray as gunpowder. Sparked, the hillside would go up in a sudden roar.

I was soon sucking air. Up ahead the steady pump of John's strong thighs made me conscious of the burn in mine—thin shanks, trembling now. He could have been down the other side and fishing by the time I reached the top, but he adjusted his pace to mine.

A western tanager appeared in a pine; his head glowed like a live coal in the dark foliage.

The descent was an easy mile. At the bottom we were blessed by the appearance of green meadow through trees on the left.

"That's it," John said. "The upper section's six or seven miles farther on."

The wide sky was a jaundiced smoky haze. Vague in the distance, a fisherman waist-deep in grass cast repeatedly to the general green. We stood on a gravel bar, looking up the creek. The still water shone strangely dark in the sick light. Beyond a near bend, a seam in the grass revealed the snaking loops of the channel as far out as the distant fisherman. John waded to the other side, crossed a wide meander, and dropped down out of sight. I moved up to the end of the bar and assembled my fly-rod. After a while I began to see trout, big fish lying along the shaded bank. From the grass I snatched a grasshopper, flung it hard toward the other side. It sat, then wiggled, then *slurp*. I selected a Dave's hopper that John had tied, cast to the ripples. The imitation floated undisturbed. I cast again, then moved up, fished from pool to pool, waded back and forth from one side to the other, gravel bar to gravel bar, winding through the esses. From creek level I couldn't see over the grass. When at last I stepped up onto the bank, it took me a minute to locate John. He was moving across the meadow, maybe a half mile away. The haze made it hard to tell. The other fisherman was gone.

Changing flies had eaten up my tippet. I sat down to tie on a new one. The water was so still and clear that I went to 6X, as fine as horsehair, but in that bleak light I could hardly see the monofilament, much less tie it to the stiff thick end of leader. Mosquitoes fed unmolested on my hands, flies buzzed around my head, and three times the blood knot failed. I needed stronger glasses. I stood up and flexed my fingers, tried again, and got it. The knot snugged tight. I tied on a fly—the pattern seemed not to matter anymore—moved upstream and cast. By one of those mysteries that convince you of unfriendly gods, the leader snarled in a rat's nest of wind knots. I gathered it in, trying not to cry, clipped it off, and set out across the meadow toward John.

Thunder grumbled overhead, rebounded among the mountains. Fine ash sifted down, flecking my forearms. I felt exposed and solitary in that expanse of grass and brown sky.

The meadow was an unlikely place to surprise a grizzly. If a bear can see or hear a person from far enough away to avoid him, you can almost count on its doing that, unless it's guarding a carcass. But everything about that afternoon—the brown sky and drifting ash, the threat of storm, and the ache in my legs and shoulders—unsettled me. Walking was hard in the thatched grass, and despite knowing better I felt the often-noted tingling sense that had caused Billy Claypoole to turn in the saddle and look back over his shoulder.

One value of feeling stalked in the high country of Yellowstone, assuming you survive it, is to be reminded that, despite the buffering effects of technology, we still live under the terms of the old dispensation. Nature can kill us quickly and easily. Not only can but sometimes does. The difference between the bear and such blind forces as fire, flood, and weather is that the bear means to, and that's where he earns his name: *Ursus horribilis*. An attack by a grizzly makes personal again something that we have long since depersonalized.

By personal I mean the kind of relationship to nature that we see in the old Inuit woman who, knowing that she can no longer contribute to the life of the family, decides one day to stay behind, alone on the ice, and wait for *nanook*. She may be afraid, but she has spent her whole life, which may not have exceeded fifty years, preparing for that rendezvous.

From where I stood the Slough Creek meadow looked as primordial as the Pleistocene. In the distance a pair of sandhill cranes sailed low through the dirty air, necks outstretched, squawking their primitive complaints. I was closer in age to fifty than to forty and feeling every year.

In shouting distance of John now, I came upon a silvered log in the tall grass near the creek. He had dropped his daypack and his rod case beside it, giving the log a look of home, of camp. It was a place to sit and rest, to drink water and eat the cheese and crackers he had brought. I dropped my gear next to his and plopped down. In a minute or two I would rummage through his pack, but first I would watch him cast.

Holding the flyrod high in his right hand to keep from snagging the tall grass behind him, he was false-casting in long, tight loops. I waited for the cast itself, but he continued to let out line, increasing the length of the loop until I thought he would surely lose his rhythm, but he kept it in the air—all that line in sinuous calligraphy—and then his arm extended and the line shot forward, flinging the tiny fly. From where I sat grass screened the creek, but I completed the presentation in my mind, admiring the floating fall of the fly—a hopper, I supposed—to the shaded water on the other side. When nothing hit, he lifted the line off the water and, false-casting all the way, moved farther upstream. I didn't know whether he had caught any fish or not, but he was showing both patience and purpose, moving like a man who knows what he's doing.

In view of the possibilities a boy might fall prey to, I was pleased that John had chosen to learn to fish for trout on flies he tied himself, that he had suffered himself to be imprinted by the landscape of Yellowstone. Observing the development of strength and skill in your children makes it easier, I should think, when your time comes to go out on the ice and wait for the bear. I could have spent the rest of the afternoon watching him cast, for he was better at it now than I would ever be, but just then his rod jerked. He had one on. I grabbed my camera and hurried toward him, flushing a hail of grasshoppers.

Holding the rod high to keep the line taut, John stepped down from the bank into knee-deep water. Framed by the lens, he slowly brought the fish toward him. I clicked the shutter as the fish jumped—caught the splash, I hoped—and clicked again as John pulled it from the creek. It was a nice cutthroat, big enough to show well in the photo. With the rod still held high, John knelt, wet his hand, and took hold of the trout. *Click.* Quickly he offered his trophy to the camera—*click*—then returned it to the water, removed the fly from its lip—*click*—and released it. "Wonder how many times that trout's been caught," he said.

"A lot, I guess."

"He acted like he knew what to do. Sort of takes the edge off."

"How many have you caught?"

"That was the third. How about you?"

"Nothing. How big were the others?"

"About like that one."

The sound of a fish breaking the surface stopped us. Circles were rippling from the far bank, thirty yards upstream. John handed me his rod. "Ease on up there and catch that fish."

I tried, cast four or five times without success. Then I joined John at the log and we ate the cheese and crackers. He was annoyed that I had caught no fish—the disappointment of the professional guide in his client's failure. I told him not to feel bad, it was my fault not his, my feeling out of tune all day, and the low, warm, clear water of Slough Creek.

III

It was the summer after that that Billy Claypoole saw the grizzly. John was back at the park, this time working through a student volunteer program as a kind of adjunct ranger. Housed at the Tower Station, he spent much time in the backcountry, helping to reestablish and mark the northern boundary, but in August he was scheduled for a week of duty at the station, and I flew out to see him.

When he had two days off, he and his girlfriend Susan and I backpacked to the upper meadow of Slough Creek and spent the night in the Elk Tongue patrol cabin, but because of the fires the summer before, the Slough Creek meadow had suffered major mudslides that turned that fabled water into a slow, black soup. We fished anyway, or went through the motions, and eventually we caught a cutthroat apiece—decent trout but streaked with oily mud. Afterward, the three of us sat on the porch talking about bears, about Billy's incredible luck, and the sun went down behind Anderson Mountain.

The cabin was stoutly built, the windows shuttered, the door thick and braced. To discourage half-hearted bears, John said. A determined grizzly can get in no matter what. He had heard reports of empty cabins raided for food. I sat on the top step gazing across the wide valley to the lower slopes on the other side, trying to conjure a grizzly out of the timber into reality. Suddenly Susan whispered *look!* And there at the foot of the steps, almost close enough to touch, sat a weasel, upright on its haunches, hardly six inches tall—a lean little muscle with sewing machine teeth. The afterglow of the sun deepened the yellow of its belly and the rich brown fur along its flanks. The weasel's small wedge of a head turned once to the right and then to the left, and then with a snakelike ripple through the grass the creature was gone.

To look at a wild animal that is looking at you is to approach a mystery. That is especially true when the animal is a carnivore—something to do perhaps with the placement of its eyes in the front of its head. Even a weasel can stir the hair on your arms. During the two seconds that we held each other's gaze, energy arced across the gap.

On the hike out the next day John said he was planning to spend a few days at the end of the season backpacking along the eastern boundary, remote country he'd always wanted to see.

"By yourself?" I asked.

"Unless I can find somebody to go with me."

"You think that's a good idea? Solo, I mean?"

"I'll have a radio."

John was twenty-two. He had been backpacking in Yellowstone for the last two summers. He knew more about bears and the park than I would ever know. Whether he knew what he was getting into now was another matter. But I had said all I could.

Susan, however, had not. "Don't worry," she said. "I won't let him go by himself."

I'll be interested, I thought, to see how that turns out.

I still don't know whether it's foolhardy to go alone overnight into the backcountry of Yellowstone Park. Certainly it is risky. As a ranger back at Tower told me later, anyone can fall and break a leg or run into bad weather, especially at that time of year. Or a bear. "So generally we don't recommend it," he said. "But John handles himself pretty well."

In other words, if John wants to do it, we'll give him a radio and a permit and wish him well.

Before I left, John laid out a map and showed me where he planned to go—down the Lamar River trail past Cache Creek to the patrol cabin at the mouth of Calfee Creek, then the next day, leaving the trail, east along Calfee toward the park boundary.

"And camp where?" I asked.

"Wherever it gets dark."

"Uunh."

"I just like the idea of sleeping where nobody's ever slept before."

Anxiety gave way for a moment to pride. To pride and the disconcerting realization that John was calmly planning to undertake a thing that I would not have dreamed of, that I for all my romance with wilderness would never choose to take it on alone, without the comfort of companionship or the attention of an audience.

"Which way are you coming out?"

"North until I hit Cache Creek again, then back to the Lamar."

Three weeks after my return from Yellowstone he called to say he was about to leave. I told him to let us know the minute he got back.

For the next three and a half days I worried. It did no good to remind myself that I was being silly, that some people's sons land F-15's on pitching carrier decks in the dark. At night I lay in bed beside my soundly sleeping wife as sleepless as I had been that night on Pebble Creek. And the bear would come—the one that killed Brigitta Fredgenhagen, a young Swiss woman hiking alone in the Yellowstone backcountry in the summer of '84. I had heard the details from one of the rangers John worked with, a man who had been part the team that investigated the incident, and I had read Stephen Herrero's account in *Bear Attacks*. According to both sources, Fredgenhagen was camping alone at White Lake north of Pelican Bay. Evidence indicated that she ate a cold supper, to avoid cooking odors, and her campsite was immaculate. In other words, she did all she should have done. Yet the bear came, sometime after 10:30 they figured, on a rainy night, and dragged her by the neck (it looked like) from her tent. Park officials never found the bear, in spite of intensive effort, but biologists concluded that it was probably an animal inured to human presence by heavy hiking traffic in the Pelican Bay area. Herrero agrees and adds a couple of ideas of his own: "Being by herself may have made her an easier victim. Another possible contributing circumstance was her camp location, adjacent to a hiking trail. . . . It is well known that in the Yellowstone region grizzly bears often travel hiking trails at night." John was hiking fifteen miles to the northeast of White Lake, no distance at all for a grizzly, and the bear that killed Brigitta Fredgenhagen five years before, as far as anyone knew, was still roaming that section of the park.

The world is a dangerous place to turn children loose in. But the time comes. A week later, our daughter Sarah Jane and her roommate would be driving back from Grand Teton National Park, where they had worked that summer. Two attractive college girls risking two thousand miles of interstate. Would they be any less in danger than John on Calfee Creek? I know parents who send their sons and daughters into this world's wilderness, with or without prayer but smiling nonetheless, and never lose a night's sleep, as far as I can tell. On the day John planned to return I stayed close to the phone. It rang late that afternoon.

His report, as I expected, was abbreviated, short enough to cram onto the back of a picture postcard. Had a great trip, he said; didn't see a soul; snowing above seven thousand feet, elk bugling up and down the valleys, almost continuously; he caught cutthroat for supper, under the nose of a bull moose.

"Really? Tell me about it."

"Well, I didn't get to the patrol cabin until later than I expected. That was the one night that I could cook without having to worry about bears, and I had been counting on fish for supper, so I dropped my pack on the porch and started fishing. But it was cold and windy and looking like snow and the fish weren't hitting anything, wet or dry. Then I saw this moose. I'd seen three or four already, hiking in, but they were all cows and a long way off. This was a trophy bull and he was crossing the creek just a few yards above me. When he got to my side, he stopped. He was headed away from me but he looked back over his shoulder toward me. I figured the best thing was to act like I hadn't noticed him, and that's when I caught the first trout. I caught the next one almost on the next cast—same size as the first—and when I looked again the moose was gone. That was the first day."

Something was coming, I could feel it, but he was waiting for me to ask. "What about the second?"

"I was sitting on a rock at the edge of a meadow, taking a break. There was this open hillside across the way with a lot of boulders and big rocks, and it looked like one of the boulders was moving. From that distance it was just a large, dark, round-looking object, but I was pretty sure what it was. My binoculars were in my backpack, in one of the side pockets, and I kept fumbling to get them out and trying to keep an eye on this thing at the same time, and then it turned. It must have turned into the wind because just like that it went from dark to light, like the wind was blowing its hair back. It just flashed a light blond. And then I was sure."

"Did you see it through binoculars?"

"Not until it had already turned away. Then it moved over the hill and I didn't see it again."

"Did it see you?"

"Not at that distance."

"How far?"

"Three hundred yards? Maybe less."

Relief was what I felt first and then pride and after pride, curiosity. How had he felt? I wanted to know. Had energy arced across even the great distance he estimated, assuring him of his own life? Was three hundred yards close enough for him to count coup on the bear? He wasn't saying, and suddenly I didn't want to pry. Whatever the experience meant, it belonged to him, not to me sitting in my air-conditioned den two thousand miles away in Georgia. It was enough to know that he had gone alone and unarmed onto an elevated plain where he received as a gift the sight of a grizzly bear that looked like a boulder moving until it turned and flashed blond in the wind.

ACCORDING TO
HEMINGWAY

"Am going fishing tomorrow and write the next day."
ERNEST HEMINGWAY TO IVAN KASHKIN

GOOD FISH STORIES start with good fish. Trout is the choice of most writers, which is not surprising when you consider that trout fishing traces its ancestry back to a book. Ernest Hemingway wrote the best trout-fishing story in American literature, maybe in the world, then went fishing in the Gulf Stream and discovered that marlin are also literary fish. But it takes more than a literary fish to make a good fish story.

Hemingway wrote well about marlin fishing in *The Old Man and the Sea,* but he wrote about it best when it was still new to him, in the 1930s, in articles he sent to *Esquire*. It was during that time that he wrote to the Russian critic Ivan Kashkin, saying that concern over one's literary reputation "is all silly as hell anyway but writing isn't silly and neither is the Gulf Stream and I wish you could go out tomorrow and see it."

I am rereading those *Esquire* pieces now, not for the purpose of learning how to tell a good fish story, but in preparation for my first marlin-fishing venture.

Until a few days ago, catching a marlin never occurred to me as something I wanted to do. Then came a letter from our daughter Sarah Jane, who is spending the year in St. Thomas. From the day she arrived there, back in June, she had been begging us to come for a visit. She knew we would love the Caribbean. And if her boyfriend's parents could come at the same time, that would be a good opportunity for us to meet them. But I had been putting her off. We'd love to, I'd told her, but I really had to write. Then came the letter, thick and addressed to me. Dear Daddy, she said, the North Drop out of St. Thomas is supposed to be the best marlin fishing in the world. If y'all could come on the full moon in September, they say that's the best time of year.

She and Jefferson—the boyfriend—had talked to a charter boat captain at Red Hook; it was all lined up. They were just waiting for the go-ahead from me. Then she said it would make her so happy for me to catch a marlin. I told Jane to make the reservations. Then I started reading Hemingway.

The excitement in catching marlin, he writes, "comes from the fact that they are strange and wild things of unbelievable speed and power and a beauty, in the water and leaping, that is indescribable, which you would never see if you did not fish for them, and to which you are suddenly harnessed so that you feel their speed, their force and their savage power as intimately as if you were riding a bucking horse."

I *would* like to see something like that, whether I'm holding the rod or not. And I'd sort of like to fish in the old man's wake, though the North Drop is not the Gulf Stream and I'm too damned old for hero worship. I doubt that he would have wanted me on his boat anyway. In an article written for *Holiday* in 1954 he complains of the "inexperienced and untrained anglers" who could not catch a big fish without help from a guide and the recently invented tackle that made it easy. That's the kind of talk you expect from an expert. I've talked that way myself about once-a-year turkey hunters who pay a guide to call up a gobbler and then wonder what the big deal is.

Billy Claypoole and his guests Charlie Creedmore and Jim Meunier were certainly "inexperienced and untrained" the first time they went marlin fishing, but I think Hemingway would have approved of the way they did it. Actually, they were fishing for dolphin and wahoo, but a marlin was what they almost caught. I heard the story from each of the three, and the versions overlapped enough to blur the edges. What I know for sure is that Creedmore and Meunier went to see Claypoole, who was living for a time in St. Croix, and that the three of them went out on a commercial fishing boat owned by a Crucian Claypoole knew and they hooked a marlin that gave them a hell of a fight—a long fight—and when they finally brought it alongside, it broke free. What I remember clearly are disconnected details: how during the fight they poured water on Creedmore's head and shoulders, how when the fish came alongside they saw that the hook was hanging by a thread, how when it broke free it seemed to take forever for the shadow of the fish to pass beneath the boat. And the way the fish jumped. Again and again and again. All three talked about that.

Billy Claypoole lives in Atlanta now. I don't see as much of him as I once did, but he's good about staying in touch, especially when he's just back from hunting or fishing in Montana or South Dakota or the upper peninsula of Michigan. This time he's thoughtful enough to call before he leaves—Alaska, he says, salmon fishing. Might get in a little ptarmigan shooting on the side.

I play my trump, tell him I'll be too busy chasing marlin to give much thought to him.

"All *right*," he says. "Out of Red Hook?"

"I think that's the name."

"Great. The North Drop is the best marlin fishing in the world. And in September too."

"That's what I've heard. But listen: Don't call me when you get back. If I have a story to tell, I'll call you."

The morning we arrive at the Red Hook marina I'm wearing a T-shirt with a cartoon of Hemingway on the front—the great writer in trophy pose, rifle in the crook of his arm, one foot resting in triumph not on a fallen buffalo but a typewriter. It will remind me not to take this marlin fishing too seriously.

The mate is a young man with a brick-colored face and fleecy arms as thick as fence posts. He must wonder what he's in for. Six of us step on board the *Boobie Hatch*—Sarah Jane and Jefferson, a friend of theirs named Dave, Jefferson's father Jeff, and Jane and me. Dave is bigger than Hemingway, plenty strong enough to handle whatever hits the lure, and both Jeffs are saltwater men, accustomed to boats. But that little guy with the white beard and the silly shirt, the mate must be thinking, who does he think he is? Hope it's not him in the chair when the big fish hits.

The mate's name is Eddie, the *Boobie Hatch* a forty-five-foot sport fisherman. Like other marlin boats, it trolls four lines—two outriggers and two flat. The rods, upright in their sockets, are as thick at the butt end as broom handles, and the polished brass reels are the size of mason jars. It must be a hell of a fish we're after.

Eddie demonstrates technique. It looks complicated and he's going too fast. "Never look at the fish," he says. "You'll lose him every time. Keep the line tight. Guide it evenly back onto the spool. If the fish sounds, this is how you pump him up. Got it?"

I want to watch someone else do it first, but the other men are feeling as unselfish as I am. No one wants first turn in the chair.

We have fifteen miles to go to reach the Drop—an underwater cliff between the Caribbean and the Atlantic that is so deep, I'm told, that a sonar crossing above it will flash suddenly from a hundred and fifty fathoms to ERROR MODE. In other words, it's bottomless on the Atlantic side. Jefferson, our resident oceanographer, explains that cold water upwelling along the face of the Drop presents a banquet of plankton for small fish, which attract bigger fish, which in turn attract the great predators that rise out of the cold darkness to eat anything they want.

When the captain throttles back to trolling speed—nine and a half knots—I figure we are there. Eddie swings into action, performing complicated feats with rods and lines and lures, and I notice that four or five other boats are trolling all around us.

The kids want their fathers to catch the first fish. The senior Jeff and I each insist that the other take the chair. I win.

The sun has climbed above the bank of clouds on the horizon and is gaining strength. The water is as blue as Winslow Homer painted it. *Ultra*marine. I bet Billy Claypoole is freezing his ass off. He is fishing with two guys from Tallahassee, husbands on sabbatical, participating in that brief, ideal society of men who share a single passion and instinctively understand a hundred little unspoken things. I know. I've been there, not to Alaska but to a dozen other places where men sleep and eat under one roof, rise before daylight regardless of the weather, and take their separate ways into the woods. And I have been there in the evenings—whiskey and firelight—and heard their careful talk. There was a time, in fact, when I cherished those moments above all other times and found—I thought then—my truest joy in such fellowship. That I am here now, on this boat with my wife and my daughter and her boyfriend and his father and not in Alaska with Billy and his friends, makes me wonder if I have crossed over without noticing it into another watershed.

I am sure at least that I am where I should be. No sooner had we landed in St. Thomas than Jefferson contrived to get me off to himself and ask my permission to marry Sarah Jane. It dawned on me then that this trip was not about fishing at all, though hooks were being set all over the place.

Jefferson's father vacates the chair, invites me to sit. Because everything is still possible this early in the morning, I keep my hopeful eye on the lures, which are skipping and bouncing in the frothy wake. I am almost confident of a fish, at any moment. Three of the lures are artificial—plastic-bright teardrops trailing streamers of pink and black, green and yellow—and one is a dead mackerel. The sun climbs higher. What I'm waiting for is the thrill that comes, according to Hemingway, at such a moment as this, "when you are standing at the wheel drinking a cold bottle of beer and watching the outriggers jump the baits so they look like small live tuna leaping along and then behind one you see a long dark shadow wing up and then a big spear thrust out followed by an eye and head and dorsal fin and the tuna jumps with the wave and he's missed it."

To see something like that come up out of the water, close behind the boat—*man*. I strain in the glare for a shadow, but the lures, following at a constant distance of thirty yards, skip merrily in the white seethe, mile after mile. I'm thirsty for something cold. It's somebody else's turn.

It would be sweet to be able to call Billy when I get back and tell him I caught a marlin. Especially if it should turn out to be bigger than the one he and the others caught.

Don't be greedy, I tell myself.

I don't remember how big they said theirs was. It must have seemed monstrous on the light dolphin tackle they were using. Nor did that dinky little commercial fishing boat come with a fighting chair. What must they have thought when the marlin struck? It was Charlie who grabbed the rod and set the hook.

That would be Eddie's job on this boat, thus his fish. I mean, if I'm in the chair when it happens, how can I claim the fish if I don't drive home the hook?

Early afternoon, big Jeff in the chair. Somebody yells *fish*. I see a little splash at the lure, hardly distinguishable from the curl of white water that feathers the edge of the wake. Eddie grabs the rod, lifts it high, jerks back on it hard. "He missed it," he says.

Charlie must have thought he had snagged an old-time sea monster and made it mad. He is a strong man, played defensive end for the University of Georgia, and ten years ago he was still in good shape. But Meunier said he staggered all over the back of the boat, the rod bent double. The fish was too much for him. Meunier had to sit down with his back against the stern and brace the rod from underneath. The part people couldn't believe when Meunier told it later was that the fish stripped off line so fast the reel began to smoke; Billy had to pour water on it, and Meunier said that the water dripping from the reel onto his bare legs was hot.

I eat one of the sandwiches we brought on board and wash it down with beer. The sun bouncing off the water makes it hard to see the boats around us or to focus on the lures in the wake. I go forward and stretch out on a bunk. The queasiness I feared has not developed, but lying down with a full stomach I swing and plunge with the bow. Not much chance of getting to sleep.

I hear my name shouted out. "Get back here!"

That's Jefferson. Somebody's got a fish. I catapult from the bunk, bare feet seeking deck, and burst from the air-conditioned cabin into the brilliance, not yet fully awake. People are lounging about, loafing on the rails, exactly as they were thirty minutes ago.

"Your turn," Jefferson says.

If this young man expects to be my son-in-law, he's going to have to learn not to wake me from a nap.

I sit. Jefferson hands me a cold can of Coke, Sarah Jane a lighted cigarette. I squint against the glare, fight my way out of sleep.

I remember the Hemingway pretty clearly, image by image, if not word for word. That's where Papa had it over almost every writer I can think of, except maybe Isak Dinesen, which he admitted himself. If you have ever read "The Big Two-Hearted River," you're bound to remember the flapjack Nick folds into wax paper and slips into his pocket and the onion sandwich he eats while standing in the cold trout stream. The rendering of those sensations that awaken us into full awareness was what he was after. He achieved it not merely by the exact use of words but by a language of such true perception that the moment is not only described, it is defined, almost sanctified.

> He can see the slicing wake of a fin, if he cuts toward the bait, or the rising and lowering sickle of a tail if he is travelling, or if he comes from behind he can see the bulk of him under water, great blue pectorals widespread like the wings of some huge, underwater bird, and the stripes around him like purple bands around a brown barrel, and then the sudden upthrust waggle of a bill. He can see him slice off to the side and go down with the bait, sometimes to swim deep down with the boat so that the line seems slack and Piscator cannot come up against him solidly to hook him. Then when he's hooked he makes a sweeping turn, the drag screwed down, the line zings out and he breaks water, the drag loosed now, to go off jumping, throwing water like a speedboat, in those long, loping, rhythmic, pounding leaps of twenty feet and more in length.

Lord, I'd love to see that, but even if a fish were to strike, Eddie says not to look at anything but the line, no matter how badly you want to. Take your eye off that, lose your concentration, and you lose the fish. I would gladly trade the chair for a chance to see a marlin make its run.

Or is it that I just prefer the safety of the sidelines, the security of the balcony when the bulls come thundering down the street? The spectator can always argue that the man who is running in front of the bulls misses the show, but I wonder if that's an excuse for fear. What I fear right now is the responsibility of fighting the fish, should one strike, of doing it right—not just for the sake of my pride but for the boat and for my family. As soon as I finish my Coke, I'm going to yield this hot seat to the young man who woke me up.

And do what? Go back to reading Hemingway? Reading is just another way of watching from the sidelines, and all I would see is what Hemingway has prepared me to see, has already shown me, in fact.

The outrigger rod on my left suddenly bucks and jumps in its socket like a bolt of lightning's hit it. Eddie grabs it, steps to my right, holding it high with both hands. If there was a splash, a waggle of bill, I missed it. Eddie rears back hard on the rod, throwing himself against it, rears back again and again, hitting the fish hard. The rod bends. He thrusts it at me, and the second I touch it the power of the fish surges through my arms all the way to my shoulders. I seat the butt in the gimbal between my legs, reel singing. Eddie does something to the drag and the pitch changes. The fish is stripping line faster than I can believe, the spool diminishing before my eyes. Eddie is strapping me into the harness, hooking the ends to eyes on the big brass Penn.

Every move he makes is confident and sure—all business. This fish is important to him, but it's my baby now.

"Reel!"

The boat is backing into its wake, water flooding in at the base of the stern.

"Reel!"

I take the crank in my right hand. I can't budge it.

"Reel!"

I lean into it, crank it one turn.

"Come on now, you got to reel, man, reel now!"

I'm not going to be able to do this.

Jane tries to help, covers my reel hand with hers, lends me her strength, but Eddie takes her by the wrist, pulls her hand away. "No," he says, "you'll knock the drag loose. He can do it."

Without a guiding device to insure an even retrieve, I have to guide line with my finger, one side to the other, a lateral motion that makes the circular cranking even harder. My arm is hurting and I'm dying to look, but my job is simple—keep my eye on the spool and turn the handle as fast as I can. The others will have to see the fish for me, if it breaks water, and tell me later what it looked like. I'll tell them how it felt.

"Oh Jesus," someone says. And Sarah Jane, right behind me, "Oh my God."

I can't help it.

Far out, maybe two hundred yards, the marlin is leaping, the entire fish, bill and fin, out of the water, standing on his tail. He's bigger than I am, much bigger, and when he falls he makes a tremendous splash.

I throw my entire right side into the reel. I can concentrate now because the fish hangs still before my eyes, shaking along its great length, tail walking, walking, walking, out across the water, and I know now as I did not before, even when his power was surging through my arms, what I am connected to, despite the distance that the mind will not believe but the body does because the image imprinted on the eye behind my eyes is one with the pain in my shoulder.

The tension slackens; the reel turns too easily. Panicky, I look. The line is sagging, too much belly, but I seem still to have the fish.

"Reel, reel, reel," shouts Eddie, who stands behind me now, hands on the back of the chair, mouth at my ear.

The boat is backing too fast for me to keep up with. The handle offers no resistance, but I don't have much left. I feel wounded in the shoulder. I don't think I can last much longer. I cover my right hand with my left.

"No," Eddie says. "The drag. You can do it."

And just like that, the line is dropping straight off the end of the rod and we're on top of the fish. I check the spool. The line is bunched up too much on the left.

"Got to bring him up now," Eddie coaches. "Remember how I told you."

"Tell me again."

"Drop the rod fast, turn the handle. Then raise it up easy. Drop fast, turn, raise him easy."

I lower the tip but can't turn the handle. I might as well be hooked to a dead horse down there, God knows how deep.

Overcompensating, I jerk the rod up, lower slowly because I'm trying to crank the handle, and when I get one turn I jerk it up again.

"No," Eddie says. "You're doing it wrong. Listen now. Up slow, down fast. And reel as you're going down."

"I understand what you're saying, but it's not that easy to do."

People laugh. That boy my daughter wants to marry. But it's sympathetic laughter.

"You can do it," Eddie says.

I no longer feel my arm and shoulder.

Suddenly, the taut line angles across the water, slicing, away from the stern.

"He's coming up, he's coming up."

The line cuts an arc, the drag whines, and the pull of the fish tips me forward, almost overboard. I plant my bare feet flat and dig in. The rod is bowed, the fish has dived again, and I have nothing left. I manage one more turn.

"*Son of a bitch.*"

"Good," Eddie says. "Get mad. Fight him now."

Another turn.

"Here he comes. Here he comes. Bring him up. Bring him up."

People are moving past me on both sides, cameras aimed. Then everybody stops and I can almost hear them catch their breath.

"Oh my God. Look at that. Did you see that? Did you catch that?"

I keep my eye fixed on the reel; the spool is full.

Sarah Jane says, "Holy cow, look at the blue on the fins. It's like neon, y'all. And the stripes."

There is commotion all around me. I notice the teardrop lure, pink and black, pushed halfway up the line, Eddie, hands gloved, reaching for the leader. Jefferson is holding something that looks like a spear, poised. Cameras snick and whir.

Whatever is going on, I'm out of it now.

Then Eddie is extending his hand. "Congratulations."

I can't lift my arm. Eddie takes my hand. His feels hard, cauterized. I wish I had the strength to grip it.

Looking up toward the tower, he asks the captain, "How much?"

"Four hundred."

"Ten feet? Eleven?"

"Ten and a half."

"Congratulations," he says again, pumping my floppy arm.

I'm sprawled on a cushioned bench in front of the tower, alone, nursing a can of beer in my left hand. I still can't trust the other to make it to my mouth. We are headed south into a soft cloudy light. A full moon, chalk white in the deepening blue, hangs low in the east, and the breeze is mild. Ernest Tubb is singing on the tape deck. I turn and tell the captain that I approve of his music. His name is Don Hamilton. He wears an Amish beard, blond chin whiskers burned white by the sun. "Yeah," he says above the sound of the twin diesels, "E.T., Hank Snow, Hank senior—I like all those old boys."

There is blood on the front of my shirt, a small red splotch on Hemingway's hand, the one that grips the rifle. I wonder where that came from. Then I see. The inside of my right knee is cut in two parallel lines—just scratches but bleeding enough for ritual.

Eddie gave me a length of the thick leader. I measure the souvenir against my arm. Almost three feet.

The marlin was tagged—that's what Jefferson's spear was for—and cut loose. I signed an affidavit. The Billfish Society will be sending me a certificate, Eddie said. If I want a mount, the taxidermist can provide one without having to use any part of the fish. But even if I could afford a piece of plastic that size, I don't have a wall big enough. The leader is enough for me and the blood on the shirt and the photographs. I hope they turn out good.

Billy and Charlie and Jim Meunier finally whipped their fish and brought it to the boat, all of them agreeing that it was a mutual catch, since each had taken a turn at the rod during the hour of the fight. In fact, Meunier said that all three reached out and touched the leader, to count coup, but I don't see how that could be; according to Billy, Charlie was holding the rod and the Crucian captain was screaming from the tower, "Gaff him!" and Billy said that before he knew it he had the gaff in his hand and he could see that the hook was hanging by the thinnest ribbon of tissue and the tissue was already looking dead and whitish, and for the briefest second he hesitated, irresolute, who had never known an uncertain moment in his life—not in the presence of game—and that's what cost them the fish. When Billy did strike, he miscalculated—all three understood without having discussed it that none of them wanted to kill the fish but the captain was yelling, "Gaff him," so Billy tried but the motion or the touch of the gaff reenergized the fish and he swam under the boat, and that's when Charlie should have come to the side and lowered the rod to the fish, but instead he stayed put, rod up, line tight, and he should have known better because he had done more saltwater fishing than the others, and suddenly the line went slack and there was nothing on the other end. It was not that the fish pulled loose. The line was cut. Against the screws, they figured, when the fish swam under the boat. Meunier said he couldn't believe how long it took for the shadow of the marlin to pass completely underneath them, and Charlie said you could see it grow smaller and smaller as it sank.

The captain was upset. According to Billy, he said, "At least the sharks will get him," and Billy understood for the first time that the Crucian saw that fish as the enemy.

Hemingway never released a marlin in his life that I know of, but neither did he mount a trophy on his wall. There were markets in Havana and Key West in those days, and his mate Carlos Guiterrez called marlin "the bread of my children." But if I understand *The Old Man and the Sea,* what happens to the marlin in the end doesn't matter anyway (except to the marlin). Fish market, sharks, or air-brushed plastic on the wall—they all get away. The fish is the very thing you cannot keep.

That's one way of explaining why Hemingway told stories; it explains too why for him the story lives not in the plot but in the image—those blessed moments when we emerge dazed from the cocoon husk of ordinariness to find ourselves connected to life.

What happened when Jane and I returned to Atlanta is not the kind of thing good writers end a story with because it was just too neat.

But it really happened, you protest.

Doesn't matter, the critic says, the fact that it happened doesn't make it true.

I don't care, you say. I'm going to tell it anyway.

The plane arrives at 11:30 P.M., four hours late. We enter baggage claim sleepy and eager for home, still two hours away, and damn if that's not Billy Claypoole, standing right there, looking in spite of a pink pullover and baggy khakis like a reserve air force officer just back from salmon fishing in Alaska.

We clasp hands, each of us knowing that neither is willing to call this coincidence.

"I have one question," I say. "Did you catch four hundred pounds of salmon?"

Billy looks puzzled for maybe a half second. Then: "All *right*. Did you really?"

"And one more. How much did y'all's weigh?"

He smiles apologetically. "Five hundred. Plus."

I'm not surprised. They all said it was big.

"I didn't realize how big he was," he continues, "until I went to gaff him. He was lying on his side and I could see his head and bill but the body and tail were angled down into the water. Then, just as I went to gaff him, the whole fish rolled to the surface, and I think that's what made me hesitate. I mean the size of him just stopped me dead."

The only time I saw mine was when he jumped and that was

about two hundred yards out—too far to see any color but you could see the dark upper parts and the silver flanks and you could see the dorsal fin and the bill and the way he stood on his tail and walked across the water shaking himself up and down, and all the time he seems like more than just a fish because you're connected to him, to all that power, and you can feel it in the tension of the line and the ache in your arms—it's just indescribable.

Part 3

INHERITANCE OF HORSES

*Included in this property at the present time are my horses,
and horse equipment, including harness, saddlery, truck, etc. If
my said wife wishes to make disposition of said livestock by
gifts to my children or grandchildren, it is her property
to do with as she pleases.*
Last Will and Testament of JAMES P. KILGO, July 1944

I

JIM KILGO loved a spirited horse and he drove with a heavy
foot. You may think I'm mixing metaphors, but those are literal
facts. When he was fifty-two, his friend Bob Lawton told him
to "take things more quietly, strive for inward peace, make the
world your brother, and you will live to be as old as a cypress
tree." But Jim was too revved up. To me he left his name, five
hundred dollars, and an L. C. Smith shotgun engraved with our
initials. Only four at the time, I have been haunted ever since,
longing to recover him, I guess, by gaining a sense of the man
as he was. But how am I to do that? I remember just enough to
know that I knew him, to know that he knew me—too little to
go on but far too much to forget.

Memory begins, we are told, when a child learns to talk,
for language is the medium by which sensation imprints itself
as image upon the mind. In one of my earliest memories I am
being lifted from behind by the armpits that I might see into a
stall where a mare has just foaled. Without a name for what I

must have smelled, I recall only the snuffling sounds of the big horse in the darkness and the colt lying small and dark in the dim hay. Another memory from the same period: buggy whip and socket, which means that someone may have spoken that new word—socket—at the instant I discovered how neatly the hole received the handle. I also remember the hearty smell of just-ground cornmeal sliding down a smooth wood chute and dust motes in the sunlight that came through the window of the mill and the warmth of the meal in the barrel when I buried my arms in it up to my elbows. I cannot date these events with precision, but they must have occurred before Christmas of 1944, when I was three and a half years old, because each involves my paternal grandfather, the man I called Pop, and in January of '45 my family moved to New Jersey and I never saw him again.

For at least a year up until that time I was with him almost every day. So you'd think that I'd remember the man as well, the smell of his shaving soap, the rasp of his jaw against my cheek, the tickle of his voice in my ear. But I don't. Photographs merge with stories I heard, causing me to think I do, but in fact only one impression remains. I don't know the year or the season, but the time of day was just after dark. We came in from outside, I in his arms; he took me over to the big desk in the sitting room where he kept a bottle of Jergens lotion, and he rubbed the lotion on our hands, mine small and slippery in his. The part I don't remember was how our clothes must have smelled like horse.

My grandparents' house—an imposing white facade— looked straight down the middle of the street where we lived, one block away. If you walked out in front of our house, you could see all the way up the avenue of oaks to their front door. Here's what I've been told: While I was still an infant, Pop would appear whenever it suited him, day or night, swoop me up from my crib, and take me with him. I was his first grandchild. My mother thinks he considered her and my father too inexperienced to take proper care of a baby, that he really thought that I, like everything else with his name on it, belonged to him. When I had my tonsils out, it was to his house that I was taken to convalesce.

As soon as I could walk, he took me almost every day after work to his horse farm out on the edge of town—a long, white stable sheltered by tall pines, a log smokehouse, and fenced riding rings, where grooms and stable boys exercised his fine saddlebreds, and a flock of sheep grazed in the open places. On Sunday afternoons Pop would hitch a horse to his buggy, and with me sandwiched between my grandmother and him we would drive to the park, an undeveloped tract of municipal property of which he had been named commissioner, while a line of automobiles stacked up behind us, honking their horns. At least once he must have taken me up to his gristmill in the next county, for I certainly remember the cornmeal.

And here's what the photographs show: a handsome saddlebred groomed to a high gloss, posing before a white fence with a solemn three-year-old perched on its back. There are a dozen or more like those—different days, different horses—but only one of this: Jim Kilgo mounted, in profile, as erect as a knight in armor.

Just before Christmas of 1944 my father, a lieutenant jg in the navy, received orders to report to a base in New Jersey. He wanted to take us with him—my mother and sister and me—but Pop said no. It was foolish to take Caroline and those babies up north where people were rude and the ground was covered with snow. Though thirty-two years old, my father was still intimidated by Pop, but in this matter he stood his ground. The day after Christmas Pop called my mother aside and told her to talk sense to John; he was acting like a fool, selfish and irresponsible. Whereupon that gentle lady—only twenty-five years old and by temperament unsuited to dissension—told her formidable father-in-law that her place was with her husband, that she would follow him wherever he went, that she trusted him absolutely, and that she was not going to let Pop say those things. She was crying by the time she got that out and Pop was too. They embraced and cried some more. They cried because Pop's other son, Bob, had been fighting in the Pacific since 1942 and because it had been a long time since anyone had heard from my mother's skinny little brother, fighting in the Belgian snow, and because nobody knew where they were sending John. Gaining control of himself, Pop said, "I'm so glad you love my boy."

Some of the people in New Jersey were rude, slamming the door in my mother's face when, with two small children in her arms, she appeared on foot to answer their ad for an apartment, and Pop was right about the snow too. Before that winter was over, I dictated a letter to him in which I told him that I had seen an upside-down house on the beach (my mother added in parentheses that she had no idea what I was talking about), and that I had boots for walking in the snow. The letter he wrote in response has been lost in recent years, but I remember that he said he knew exactly what an upside-down house was. Because he and I were charter members of the Jimmy Club, we understood many things that grown-ups had long since forgotten. And he praised boots. Every man should have a good pair of boots. He had once owned a fine pair for bird hunting, but they had disappeared; he had an idea that my Uncle Bob might know what became of them because he and Pop had the same size foot and Bob liked to hunt birds too.

Germany fell in April, I turned four in June, and my father was discharged from the navy without having been sent overseas. By the first week of July we were packing for home. I'm sure my parents fanned my excitement. We would be seeing Mama and Pop again, and I would soon be big enough to have a horse of my own. I clearly remember my father's disappointment over our having to miss by one day Pop's Second Annual Darlington Horse Show. He had started it the year before, in July, and this one was to be even better. "He's added a hunter class this year," Daddy said.

"What's that?" I asked.

"A hunter is a horse that jumps. Over fences and things."

We spent no more than a night or two in Darlington, which I have no recollection of, and then left for my mother's parents in Greenwood. No sooner had we arrived than a call came from Darlington. Pop had suffered a ruptured appendix; he was going into surgery. My father left immediately.

Pop stood the operation well, recovered quickly, and began to complain about the nurses. "Tell the doctor I'm ready to go," he instructed my father. "Marco [a black employee] can look after me better than these people." But when Daddy went to the hospital the next day, the doctor stopped him in the hall and told him that his father was very sick. Peritonitis. The day after that, Daddy called Greenwood to say that Pop was dead.

As though I were struck dumb by that loss, my memory of the year between the death of my grandfather and my fifth birthday is a strip of overexposed film. I have been told that my parents not only decided against taking me to the funeral, they didn't even tell me the reason for their leaving my sister and me in Greenwood. But I must have seen in the anguish on my father's face that something very bad had happened. That's what my grandmother thought. After I was grown, she told me that when my parents left I stood at the window sobbing for a long time and didn't stop until I fell asleep.

On the first anniversary of Pop's death my uncle Bob Kilgo wrote to his mother describing his feelings upon returning from the Philippines in October of '45; the joy of entering that house after four years of thinking he would never see it again was muted as he stepped into the wide front hall and found it empty of his father, and he wondered for a moment if there was any point in coming home. So it must have seemed to me. I don't know how they explained Pop's absence, the emptiness of my once familiar world, nor whether they ever took me back to the stable. The next thing I knew, they were telling me that Pop's horses had been sold at auction. Our horses. I was angry. With Pop gone, they should have checked with me first. I resented them for lacking the interest (and the money, they said) to maintain the stable until I was old enough to take it over.

The gristmill with its beautiful pond and six hundred and forty acres of woods went to Uncle Bob, who sold it a year later to pay his way through law school. My father took me with him when he and Bob went up to clean out a cabin on the property. A mounted bobcat perched on the mantel above the fireplace. Its eyes burned in that dim room, and I was not convinced it was dead.

The first time I saw my father cry I was in high school. He was going through a stack of old letters and came upon one his father had written to him when he was in college. As he read it, he began to weep. Putting the letter away, he said to me, "My daddy was the greatest man I ever knew."

He had been telling me that since Pop died, illustrating his devotion with stories about Pop's great heart, his generosity and compassion, his fearlessness. "I have seen him get up on a half-broken colt without a second's hesitation. It's a miracle one of those horses didn't kill him." What I heard like a refrain to these stories was how much my grandfather loved me. "He had you on a horse before you could walk," Daddy said. Then he laughed. "You were too young to remember this—you couldn't have been more than three years old—but when

Daddy held that first horse show—he was the grand marshal, of course, leading the procession—when he came around to where we were sitting, he stopped the show and had me lift you up to him, and then he paraded around one more time with you in the saddle in front of him."

At the same time I was learning from my parents that God loved me too, that Pop was with Our Father in heaven, that Pop would be proud of me. I knew that Daddy worshiped Pop. He also worshiped God. I saw that every Sunday, Daddy sitting on the aisle end of the front pew where Pop had sat, head bowed in prayer. The day came when I asked my father why he had named me Jimmy instead of John Simpson Kilgo, Jr. "Because I loved my father more than myself," he said. Somehow that answer caused my sense of Pop to coalesce with my idea of God to produce a blurry presence that hovered in sunlit space just beyond the edge of the world, just beyond the grasp of conscious memory. Pop would be with me always. Yet what I continued to feel most keenly was his absence from the house on St. John's Street.

One day when I was seven or eight, while exploring an upstairs storage room, I found leaning against the wall a large board, like a bulletin board, maybe four feet by six; it was festooned with ribbons, crowded and overlapped—ribbons of deep blue and purple, scarlet, white, pale green and yellow, a richness of ribbons and rosettes that proclaimed the beauty of the horses that might have been mine.

Two or three years later I started camping with friends out at Pop's old stable. It was smaller than my half-remembered, glorified impressions, of course—three stalls and a tack room on the front, three stalls and a room with a woodstove on the back—and pines had grown up in the old riding rings. I prowled with a soft foot through the dark interior, careful not to disturb the ghosts of men or horses. Dust lay thick on every surface, and the walls were gauzy with cobwebs, but we found old manure in the stalls, a few mysterious vials of medicine in one of the rooms, and bales of hay in the loft. Unable to summon into memory the place as I knew it must have been, when stable boys led sleek bays and sorrels down the covered passageway, and from somewhere out of sight a stallion announced his intentions to the world, I felt betrayed, victim of a cosmic injustice, as though that stable were the ruined palace of my forefathers and I the disenfranchised prince. If only Pop had lived, I anguished a thousand times, my life would have been blessed with horses.

My father's nature was more like his mother's, steady and somewhat retiring, but I could whip it into a frenzy. The crowd I was running with at sixteen and seventeen was too wild-eyed to suit him; I resented his objections as stuffy and small-minded and chafed against his overbearing authoritarianism. Differences of opinion on topics ranging from church to movies to civil rights often erupted into bitter argument at the supper table. In the heat of battle one day, he said, "You think I'm conservative, you ain't seen nothing. You should have known *my* daddy. If he had lived, the two of you would have clashed on everything."

The truth of that—self-evident and undeniable—struck me like a blow to the midsection. I had already dispensed with God—at least the God of the Methodist church in Darlington; the bond between my father and me was being tested to its limits. And now Pop, who had hovered throughout my childhood like a daily cloud and a nighttime pillar of fire, was suddenly not there. He was on Daddy's side, the third person of a triumvirate of patriarchal authority that did not approve of me.

What kept me from grieving too heavily over the loss was my increasing disapproval of him. As I grew into adulthood, my father's stories of Pop took on an edge—and a darker tone

Even when Daddy meant to praise him, something else asserted itself, wanting to be told. To illustrate Pop's integrity, for example, he said that Pop went to Detroit on business once, and while he was there his bank in Darlington went under, invalidating the check with which he had paid his hotel bill. Immediately, he arranged by telephone to deposit funds in another local bank, but before he returned home, that bank too had closed its doors. Though Pop lost a considerable amount of money in those collapses, he nevertheless found a way to pay the hotel in Detroit. But what was the nature of his business in Detroit? In 1919 Pop had opened one of the first Chevrolet dealerships in South Carolina. In the year the banks failed—probably 1932— the regional office of General Motors sent an auditor around to check the books of local franchises. Pop refused to admit him. It was not that he had anything to hide; he just considered his books his business. When the man insisted, Pop threw him out on the street. Within a week Pop received a letter from Detroit revoking his dealership. Apparently, he had to go north to eat crow.

One of my heroes in high school was our family doctor, Mac Wilcox. My father did not altogether approve of Doctor Mac, at least not as a model for his son, and he told me one day that Pop and Doctor Mac had been bitter enemies. When I asked why, he said that Mac had once brought his car in to have some work done—a car he had bought from Pop—and asked the mechanic if they could let him use a demonstrator. "An entirely reasonable request for a doctor," my father said. "When the mechanic went in to ask, Daddy said, 'Who in the hell does Mac Wilcox think he is that I should have to provide him transportation?' And Mac heard him say it. Needless to say, Mac never bought another car from Daddy, and I don't blame him. That was the kind of fool thing Daddy was capable of, and it hurt him."

Praise of Pop's careful economy might prompt Daddy to tell of the infamous black book, a ledger in which Pop kept scrupulous household accounts; if someone gave my grandmother a hen, say, or even a jar of peach preserves, he would deduct the value of that item from her grocery allowance. "Daddy was too hard on Mama," my father would say. As though that statement had stirred up a sediment that had long lain dormant on the floor of his memory, he would add, "I hate to say it but Daddy could be real ugly at times." Then he would tell of the day Pop came in tired from work to find my grandmother's bridge club in his living room and flew into a rage. Damned if he would have his home turned into a henhouse, he stormed, and he ran the women out.

By then I was more interested in my father's attitude toward Pop than I was in Pop himself. It was easy to conclude that Daddy had long resented his father's harsh authority without being able to admit it, that only now, in middle age, was he having to face that anger. He was doing it by telling stories, and it seemed appropriate somehow that I should be the one he chose to tell them to. In any case, my awareness of my grandfather's darker side coincided with my growing exposure to unredeemed human nature, in me as well as in others. That should have made me more tolerant of his flawed and cracked clay feet, but instead I convicted him of the attitudes I most despised—legalism, bigotry, just plain meanness—and I concluded that he must have been an abrasive son of a bitch, not worth losing sleep over.

Yet I did lose sleep, from a recurring dream in which I arrive after a journey, at a house with many large rooms—not unlike his house in Darlington nor unlike his stable but different from either—and find him there. I don't recognize him at first because I have not expected to find him, but he always knows me, and in that recognition there is laughter and delight and the beatitude of complete satisfaction, all questions answered.

Yet waiting for me, every time I awoke, was the stern face in a small gold frame on the table—the face of a man who kept close accounts with the world—and I would feel again the old longing for all that I had lost.

II

I can't remember a time when I didn't know that Pop and my other grandfather, Bob Lawton, whom I called Doc, were good friends. As I grew into an awareness of it, I must have taken it for granted. We *were* all family, weren't we? My father's younger brother—Uncle Bob just home from the war—was Robert Lawton Kilgo, so named by Pop in honor of his friend. When I learned that Pop and Doc had roomed together in college, I still was not surprised. If their children loved each other enough to become my father and mother, I reasoned, then of course Pop and Doc must have known each other in college. When I was older, Daddy told me a story that had become part of our family lore. One morning during their college years Pop came in from class and threw himself rambunctiously upon Doc, who was sitting in a chair whittling. Doc turned his sharp knife upon himself, and the blade entered his navel, puncturing the artery. Blood spurted like water from a garden hose. Drenched red all down the front, Pop rushed out into the street, seeking help. By chance a doctor was passing the house, on his way to his office. He performed surgery immediately, the patient laid out on a table, and saved Doc's life.

Whether Daddy intended it or not, I concluded that Doc had loved Pop so much that he'd turned the knife upon himself rather than stab his friend.

During the years that I knew him, Doc was confined to bed by a chronic gastrointestinal illness that had caused malnutrition and tooth loss, and by the debilitating effects of malaria, and by the periodic onslaught of migraine headache. One problem was always leading to another. At times he was critically ill. Yet through all his suffering—mental anguish as well as physical pain—he maintained a sweetness of spirit that drew people to his bed—strangers as well as friends—from all over the state. As much as he loved to talk, he preferred to listen, focusing full attention on his guest, be it Billy Graham or the yardman next door. His kindness was a balm to hurting people, and his hands were beautiful. As I learned of Pop's irascible, intolerant nature, his bigotry and his pettiness, I found it hard to believe that he and Doc had been so devoted to each other, particularly that Doc had found anything lovable in Jim Kilgo. One day I asked my father what he thought.

Daddy said he didn't know. Two more different men had never lived. And then he told this story.

After he was grown, Daddy had ridden with Pop one day up to the gristmill. There they came upon a tattered old black man gathering fallen sticks for firewood. Pop cussed out the poor old fellow, told him never to set foot on that property again, and then he made him dump the sticks he had gathered.

A man could go to hell for that, I thought.

"Can you imagine what Doc would have said to that?" Daddy asked.

"Did you say anything?"

"My father did not tolerate opposition," Daddy said. "But if anyone could have stood up to him, it would have been Doc."

If a man is known by his friends, then Doc's love speaks well of Pop. Doc rarely spoke of him to me except in terms of general praise. But eventually I acquired their correspondence— the love he spoke to Pop himself, scrawled in an almost illegible script, and Pop's words to him, neatly typed. The letters had lain buried since 1945, in a forgotten drawer in the house on St.

John's Street, but they came to light when my parents sold the place, and my father gave them to me—a stack of envelopes simply addressed *Jas. P. Kilgo, Darlington, S.C.* or *Robt. O. Lawton, Greenwood, S.C.,* each decorated by that violet three-cent Jefferson. I glanced at them, read at them, but, deterred by Doc's cramped hand, I put them away in a drawer of my own.

Years later I brought them out. My father had entered the long, slow decline from which he would never recover, and maybe I wanted to read them while he was still around to answer questions. But something else was going on as well: Having reached the age at which my grandfathers began the correspondence, I almost felt included. In a way, it seemed, they were writing to me.

The first letter, Jim to Bob, is dated 1932, a rough year for a man with a family. Jim at forty-seven was a solid citizen of Darlington—owner of the Chevrolet dealership, park commissioner, Sunday-school teacher, and chairman of the board of stewards at Trinity Methodist Church. Some people thought he resembled Will Rogers, for he had a lock that hung across one side of his forehead and a crooked grin that might remind you of the comedian, but he was not smiling much. A photograph from the period shows a face worn with anxiety and hardened in its resistance to adversity, thinning hair and a jaw gone fleshy. In the depths of the Depression, he was working feverishly to meet expenses, two of which were tuition payments to Wofford and Converse colleges for John and his daughter Mae, and, judging from his letters, he was struggling with his private depression. On a Sunday afternoon in the summer he and his wife Ola drove over to Columbia to see Bob and Anne Lawton. Though too ill to hold a pastorate, Bob was teaching Bible and English literature at Columbia College, receiving practically no salary, scraping by on beans and rice. The visit was a good one for both men. Afterward, Bob, lacking the strength to write, dictated to his daughter Mary a letter to Jim. His response reveals a gloomy state of mind.

> Your letter and thoughtfulness were greatly appreciated by me. My wife also thinks it very nice of you to write us, and especially is that lady appreciative of the good judgement of your beautiful daughter [who must have appended a complimentary note of her own]. I am so broken these days in looks and fortune, if not nervously and mentally, that she finds it necessary to make excuses for me. So when anybody comes along and says anything nice about me, to that extent she feels that the burden of a feeble husband is lifted, not from me but from her shoulders.

> Your letter though was a real inspiration. I don't know really how I feel these days. Living has been so hard, and meeting ordinary business obligations well nigh impossible with such terrible losses which we have been forced to take over a year or so. Business has never had any attractions for me, other than the attractions it might have for anybody, and they are rather mean. But having cast my lot in that direction rather involuntarily some years ago, I can't do anything else, and though at times I have puffed myself up with the idea that I had performed where others could not have, the achievement is not worth what it cost. . . . I have felt that life, if confined to business, was not worth living.

Clearly, Jim had entered upon some crisis of the mind and spirit. In the same somber mood, he wrote to his son John, who was a senior at Wofford College:

> I have always held to the theory that no man can amount to a hill of beans who wants to be popular, who wants to be with the crowd, who thinks no thoughts but the thoughts of the crowd, and who has no ambition or aspiration above the level of the crowd. But this idea, while sound, I am sure, can carry one to

the wrong extreme. I am sure in this sense I have erred. I have been rather exclusive in my desires for association, not caring for many people. Not that I have anything against any man or woman, but I haven't the time or taste for them.

Jim's impatience with anything he considered frivolous or trivial and his susceptibility to depression stamped his personality from the beginning. Writing to Bob in 1941, he confessed, "My own childhood was not the happiest thing I ever knew. Somehow I didn't seem to fit into things, and at altogether too early an age I became too serious."

Jim blamed his father for that. The elder Kilgo was a prominent Methodist preacher, known throughout the Conference as "dear old Doctor Jim." But he was anything but dear to his oldest son. Explaining himself to Bob, Jim wrote,

> When I grew up I was taught to believe that everything I did was wrong and that children were a kind of necessary evil and responsibility that weighed heavily on their parents, and such a thing as any kind of encouragement to make life seem a bright thing never came to me, except when it could be "slipped" around the corner, probably, by my mother; but then nothing must be said about it. I resented it from the bottom of my soul and was never an hour without the consciousness of this feeling of resentment. In fact, to this day I'm not over it.

By contrast, his devotion to his mother approached adoration. In a letter to John he said, "You were old enough to remember Muddie [the children's name for Jim's mother], and you have always known how passionately your dad loved her." But her understanding of her difficult son could not undo the damage. Taught by a harsh, unloving father that God is the Father of us all, Jim emerged from adolescence miserably yet incorrigibly religious, a rebellious but abject believer in a God he could neither love nor deny, or, more accurately, in a God whose love for him he could not believe because it had not been mediated to him by the one man who had that responsibility.

Such was the boy Bob Lawton met when he transferred to Wofford College in 1903. Years later Jim's college friend Milton Ariail recalled that Jim "was then, as he was throughout his life, dynamic, foursquare, tense and unafraid. . . . His high-strung nature was deeply concentrated. He never sought width but he narrowed his furrow and went deep." The picture of Jim in the class photo confirms Ariail's recollection. On the front row of the stiffly posed junior class, he is the one who stands out, one foot forward, his face turned to the left, leading with his jaw, refusing to blend into the crowd.

He was not the most popular boy on campus. A passage in a letter to Bob, written forty years after their college days, explains why:

> Of course you understand my raillery at your wanting to stop at every telephone pole as you walk down a street and meet any jackleg, just as any other pup has a habit of stopping at poles. Or when you find the time to listen to another prate of the values of a good garden site. That all has its place, but personally unless there is something more than a garden spot involved, I have never had the time or disposition to waste my time with such. The bane of my existence used to be getting you from the college as far as Bishop's famous corner. It may have been that telephone poles in the area were thickly set, but it invariably happened that you had to meet a P—— L——, or one of similar ilk at every pole, and I had to stand and wait until the two of you had relieved yourselves. Generally the trip to the Bishop's corner consumed about an hour. But that was your way, and I loved you in spite of it, and have never held it against you.

Bob, on the other hand, was loved by everyone who knew him. Frail, studious, and preministerial, he came not from a Methodist parsonage but from an impoverished cotton plantation on the lower Savannah River, the sixth child of a big-talking, hard-drinking father and an aristocratic mother, who, though every inch a lady, was not particularly religious. Except for his brothers, Bob's boyhood companions had been black children, some of them mulattoes sired by men he knew. By the time he arrived at Wofford he had resolved to shun whiskey, cards, profanity, and dancing. Yet his wit and generous spirit so endeared him to his classmates that they elected him president of the senior class.

If friendship develops out of mutual interests, Jim and Bob, in spite of their different personalities, shared enough to keep a conversation going into the early hours of the morning. They were both English majors, passionate about poetry; they loved outdoor sports, especially fishing and quail hunting; and according to comments in Jim's letters, they often sat up late discussing women, specifically, what it would take in a woman to make an ideal wife. But it was not until the summer after Bob's graduation that their friendship intensified into the love that would last until Jim's death. According to Jim's own account, written forty years later, Bob had been on his way through Spartanburg to Glenn Springs, a resort hotel in Spartanburg County owned by the father of the girl Bob would eventually marry. After dinner at the Kilgo home, Jim drove his friend in a buggy the ten miles out to the springs.

And on that ride, and from that date, I have always counted the beginning of a friendship which to me has meant a great force in my thinking and in my living. I remember a whole lot of things that had been pestering me that I wanted to disgorge, and you I had picked as the victim. And I have never yet stopped disgorging, good, bad, and indifferent. And it was mostly bad, on that occasion. I was really rocked, and rocked sadly, and I could not think of any possibility that it would be of any interest to any other human being, but I decided to put you to the test. That's how it happened. No use telling you what it was all about, if you do not remember. The point is I disgorged, that you put up with it, and that I have loved you with a peculiar kind of love, and felt bound in a way that I had never been bound before, and am still bound in rings of steel that show no wear or breakage.

Such frank expressions of love by one man to another were unusual even in the 1930s, but both Jim and Bob had read Victorian poetry since their school days, and both knew by heart long passages of Alfred, Lord Tennyson's *In Memoriam,* the poet's tribute to his beloved friend Arthur Hallam. In fact, it is likely that their reading of Tennyson provided them with a model for their friendship. In any case, you hear no self-consciousness, and not the slightest hint of discomfort, in their declarations of affection, though often they made a joke of it, as Jim did in his letter about the telephone poles between campus and Bishop's Corner, and as Bob did in this letter to Jim:

You bald-headed scarecrow,

Please without delay ship my pigs. I am entirely against the idea of having them associate longer with you. I do not greatly care to have them corrupted. I want reliable, energetic, serious-minded pigs that have some sort of conception of friendship and obligation, pigs that are ready and willing to travel even a long distance for a friend. It would suit me better if the pigs never saw you again. They may fall under the spell of your fascinating ways at sight. It has been that way with me through the years. People are soon deluded into turning fool about you, and remain so, and more so. That's why I have been so fool about you so long.

To those who knew him and had to live with him every day, Jim was often abrupt and impatient, especially during the years of the Depression, and he could be devastating in his criticism of unsatisfactory performance. But alone in his office on a Sunday afternoon, he spoke to Bob in a tone others were not allowed to hear:

> I have loved you long and very deeply. You have been the greatest confidant I ever had. I have had things that wracked me which belonged to me alone, but somehow I always felt better when I had shared them with you. You have been more encouragement to me than any living soul, and I really was that sentimental about you, and wanted your love and confidence so much that at times when I had not recently contacted you, I simply had to sit down to a typewriter and write you that you had to write to me that you loved me. I want you to write to me now if you can. If you can't write much, just write me that I am a great man, even if you have to lie to do it. I like to hear you say you love me because I am worth it, when I have known that I wasn't.

And Bob responded:

> You are a great heart, a great spirit, a great man. You hate piffle. You despise hypocrisy. You are strong for reality. You are an authentic hater and certainly you are an authentic lover. There is nothing small about you. None of the elements of littleness. You are a straight and hard shooter but as tender as a very gentle woman. And moreover I am in love with you. No semblance of doubt about that. And I thank God greatly for you.

Though I have enjoyed the fellowship of men and have loved four or five of them as brothers, nothing I have experienced helps me to understand the intensity of Jim Kilgo's love for Bob Lawton. It was passionate and possessive, almost exclusive, and it was abject at times in its dependency. In those ways it was more like a romantic love than a robust friendship, for friendship always has room for others. Jim himself called it "a peculiar kind of love," and when John became engaged to Bob's daughter Caroline, Jim wrote to his friend, "Well, the families are to be bound closer than you and I have been bound, which makes me very happy."

In the cloistered, provincial world of Darlington in the 1920s and '30s, I doubt that Jim had ever encountered a homosexual relationship. If he had, he would have denounced it as a perversion. If any man had been stupid enough to suggest to him that his love for Bob Lawton was sexual, Jim would have knocked him down, or tried to, and while the man was still on the ground, Jim would have informed him that Bob Lawton was incapable of even conceiving of such an abomination. And then he would have hit the man again. I'm pretty sure of that.

What I'm not sure of is how deeply and honestly Jim understood himself. That is not to say that he was a man with unacknowledged homosexual inclinations, whatever those may be, but merely to suggest that his overheated masculinity may have been a pose. Life was nothing but a contest, he said, a glorious battle to be fought by stalwart men, and he was ever hot for the fray. Men less combative he dismissed as "namby-pamby" men such as his father, I suspect. That old preacher has been remembered as a gentle, soft-spoken man, the opposite of his fiery brother John Carlisle Kilgo, Methodist bishop and president of Trinity College. Jim made no secret of his preference for his uncle, and I wonder if all his bluster was just a way of saying to his father, *I am a man now, a real man like Uncle John. If I can't earn your blessing, I will at least get your attention.*

Only with Bob could he be himself, shed the costume, and expose the weaknesses he concealed from the world. He could do that because he believed, simply and without a doubt, that Bob Lawton was the best man he had ever known—the purest, the wisest, the most Christ-like. In Bob's presence nothing less than honesty would do; if Bob could love the real Jim, there must be something to him after all. Listen:

If I had the guts you have, rotten as they are, I'd turn this world up side down. To think of the fight you have made over the years, while you cheated life as your doctor said, and to remember you only as smiling, and throwing chairs at me, and expressing continually the hope that you will be cured eventually, and thinking evil of nobody or anything, but taking the lot of suffering you have been called upon to endure as a heavenly visitation, and believing as you have in a gospel of suffering, without a murmur or complaint, but carrying on in spite of it all, all of this makes of you in deed and in fact an influence for righteousness in some of us who have known you in our humiliation from looking at such an example.

No wonder he craved Bob's approval. And counted it as blessing.

In his last surviving letter to Bob, written five months before his death, Jim spelled out the dynamics of their friendship as he understood it. He was staring sixty in the face. For the first time in his life, all three of his children were gone, young Bob somewhere in the Pacific, and he was not feeling well. On a cold, overcast Sunday afternoon he went down to his office and inserted company stationery into the Underwood. He had not been able to get to Greenwood, he said, because of rationed gas and rubber.

But I have thought of you. I have wanted to be with you, and to talk with you. Somehow, I feel not only happier, and in better frame of mind, but I also feel that I am a better man after a visit to you.

Did you ever think of the estimate that Christ placed on friendship? Of the test he layed down for friendship? Listen: "Greater love hath no man than this, that he will lay down his life for his friend. Henceforth I call you no longer servants, but friends; for the servant knoweth not what the master doeth; but I have called you friends, *for all things that I have heard of my Father, I have*

made known unto you." I have quoted from memory, but I think
it fairly accurate, at least it is accurate in meaning. Recently I had
to make a Sunday School talk in which this scripture was a part
of the printed text, and again the thinking veered around to you.
In the first place, the highest achievement of Christ on earth was
to know the Father, his best thinking, his highest aspirations, his
holiest impulses, came from the search for the Father, and his
happiest moments came as he understood that Father's will. In
other words, it was the best that he (Christ) could think, it was
his dearest possession, it was his most sacred living. *All of this I
have made known unto you,* and therefore, you are on the plain
that I can call a friend. Before that the disciples were servants.
Only to those whom we may unburden our hearts, our souls, the
best that is in us may we call friends in the sense that he called
them friends.

Then he applies the stunning implications of that paragraph
to themselves:

I remember on one occasion in Spartanburg, with Uncle John
stopped over between trains for about two hours, and in his
big, monopolizing way, he talked to the absolute exclusion of
[other guests]. When he got ready to go to his train, and told my
mother goodbye, she who had sat enthralled and intense during the whole discourse, said, "John I love for you to come to
see us, because when you leave I always feel that I know more
about God." That was a large saying, Bud, if you can appreci-
ate it. It terribly impressed me at the time, and has never left
me, and has been responsible many a time for my thinking on
other occasions. Well, those two spirits understood each other,
and knew the deeps in the other's nature, so they could be said
to be friends. So when you talk of friendship being "a thing of
the spirit world," you see that my own thinking cannot be far
from yours. The best that is in me belongs to my friend, who
will recognize it as my best, and find happiness in the fact that I
share it with him.

To the extent that Jim's mother, sitting at the figurative feet of John Kilgo, reminds us of Mary of Bethany at the literal feet of Jesus, Jim not only identified Bob with spiritual authority, but by aligning himself with the women, he acknowledged, if only subconsciously, the female in himself. She was the student, the friend, the recipient of Bob's Christ-like knowledge of the Father, and Jim seemed at peace in that role, recognizing that for all his brandishing of fists, his hurling of challenges into the teeth of the world, it was Bob, physically weak and flat on his back, who was the true fighter, hence the real man. Such moments may have been infrequent, but, as Jim said himself, they brought out the best in him and left him a better man.

Two months after writing that letter, Jim went to see Bob for what turned out to be the last time. After the visit, Bob wrote,

> But here I am running along about myself, when nothing was further from my mind when I took pen to write a line to the *best* friend I have in this world. I, too, had a gorgeous day and a noble fellowship, and your visit was an inspiration and a joy to me. Every time I see you I lament that we do not live in the same town. That would, indeed, be wonderful. We'll have to have it out in heaven. Won't we have a glorious time, Lad?

> I can't get over what a nice time you and I had together. When this war is over, and the boys come home, we must see more of each other.

> But pshaw! I must try to get to sleep. I loved you long ago and since then, and as long as I live.

In the summer of 1941, one year and a week after John Kilgo and Caroline Lawton were married, Caroline gave birth to a son. The baby arrived at three in the morning, in a hospital ten miles from Darlington. John rushed immediately to St. John's Street and woke his mother and father with the news. When daylight came, Jim went down to his office and wrote to Bob. Predictably, he strutted up and down three pages. It was true, he said, that Bob had become a granddad first, but that "was of the petticoat variety." Who couldn't do that? But when it came to "being a real granddad, I put it all over you."

From the way he raved, you would think he had authored the event himself. Incredibly, he teases Bob for being "determined to claim an interest in what Caroline and I have accomplished." What he is really trying to say is that this boy, named for him, is *their* offspring—his and Bob's—in some sense an embodiment of their love for each other.

III

If I could write Jim Kilgo into life, I might be able to recover my inheritance, but how am I to do that without a story to tell? Assemble what he left—photographs, anecdotes, even the letters; add what you know—the house, the stable, the humid summers in Darlington, the room where Doc lay sick; and even so you get nothing but collage, a hodgepodge of nouns and adjectives but not a single verb.

That's all it took—one verb—and my father could not say it. When he tried, it came out in nouns: *that business with that woman*. He was dying, slowly but without much pain, and when I went home to see him, we talked about Pop. I don't remember which of us initiated those conversations, nor do I understand what we had in mind, but I'm sure we both sensed that this would be the last time the three of us came together. Most of what he said I'd heard before, good and bad, but one day he referred in passing to "that business with that woman." He must have thought I knew what he was talking about because he offered no details, and I was afraid to ask, but the verbs he refused to speak galloped through my head.

Of all Pop's flaws, sexual impropriety seemed the least likely. Photographs show the face of a moralist, intolerant and self-righteous—a countenance uncracked by humor, unlikely to flutter hearts. I just could not believe it.

A year later, when my father was no longer even trying to get out of bed, I risked a question. "Did you tell me once that Pop had an affair or did I just imagine that?"

"You must have imagined it," he said. And that was that.

I was baffled. My father, I believe, was constitutionally incapable of telling a lie. If he said he had not told me, that's what he believed. He must have thought I'd heard it elsewhere, but he was not inclined to discuss it.

A few days after his funeral I related that incident to my sister Caroline. Her mouth fell open. Daddy had told her the whole story, she said. She had naturally assumed that he had told me too.

The affair took place while our father was in college, or maybe the year after he graduated. That would have been in 1932 or '33, which was the year Pop's father died, when Pop was forty-eight. The woman was young, perhaps a widow— Caroline wasn't sure—but in any case she was having a hard time financially, and Pop had tried to help her. Daddy had not said how long it lasted, but while it did, they met at the cabin at the millpond—the one with the bobcat on the mantel. Eventually, my grandmother found a note from the woman. (Was she emptying his pockets before taking his suit to the cleaner, or had he, like so many guilty men, carelessly left it out where she would find it?) Devastated, my grandmother called the children together and told them she wanted to divorce their father, a desperate measure at that time and place. They were sympathetic but begged Ola to consider the scandal. From that day until the end of his life Pop slept alone in an upstairs bedroom.

I had known that. Daddy had told me more than once that

Pop usually went to bed around midnight but lay awake reading and smoking until four o'clock in the morning, a practice he
would not have followed if Ola had been trying to sleep in the
bed beside him. Daddy said he'd smoke a pack of cigarettes between supper and the time he went to sleep; every morning the
hearth in his room was littered with butts. Now I knew why.

What I don't know—cannot imagine—is how the whole
thing started. Everything I've learned about Jim Kilgo con-
vinces me that he was one of those southern gentlemen who
confuse romantic idealism with morality, believing that fine
moral scruples keep them faithful to their wives when in fact
they are too chivalric to go to bed with a woman to whom they
cannot commit themselves. That doesn't stop them from be-
coming emotionally entangled, but they are careful to choose
women who are unavailable—too young, too principled, or too
married themselves. That way, they can enjoy the anguish of un-
consummated passion without risking the consequences. The
weakness of that fortress is the protective door—it's locked
from the outside. What happens when the woman decides to
open it?

It's possible, of course, that I'm wrong, that Jim was just
a middle-aged man on the make, but I don't think so. He
had never been casual about any relationship, and he was too
morally nervous to be casual about sex. He was also vulnerable,
as are most men his age, to an attractive younger woman; more-
over, he was exhausted, mentally and physically, from working
day and night through the darkest year of the Depression; and
for the first time in his life he was nobody's son.

Whether one regards the death of one's father as loss or lib-
eration, it is bound to remind him, especially if he is around the
half-century mark himself, that his turn is next. I'm not trying
to make excuses for my grandfather but to understand how it

could have been that he might have said to her one day that he was tired, that he'd love to spend an afternoon by his millpond, get his mind off things, it was such a quiet, peaceful place; he wished she could see it; and she said, show it to me.

It's funny what you remember. I could not have been older than five when Daddy and Uncle Bob took me up to the millpond to clean out the cabin, but I remember, in addition to the bobcat, phonograph records, stacks of them, with red labels, RCA. Whatever the music was, I bet the records were hers, that she brought them to the cabin and cranked the old Victrola while he got a fire going.

I wish I could hear that music, or read the note that must have been sweet enough to incriminate. I wonder if she made him laugh. But all I know for sure is the verb. And its consequences, which throw new light on Jim's letters to Bob, defining and clarifying his need for Bob's acceptance. Listen again:

> I have had things which wracked me which belonged to me alone, but somehow I always felt better when I had shared them with you.
> . . . just write me that I am a great man, even if you have to lie to do it. I like to hear you say you love me because I am worth it, when I have known that I wasn't.

According to my mother, John somehow learned of his father's affair before the note came to light; she said it almost killed him. Whether he acted on it or not, she didn't know, but, being young and devoted to his mother, he blamed his father and held it against him. John's anger and disappointment must have broken Jim's heart. In the letter prompted by John's engagement to Caroline, written a few years after the affair, Jim said,

> As you have known, John has always been a kind of weakness with me. I have studied the kid from his infancy, and have always

tried to establish and keep the most intimate relationship that could exist between a father and son. John is not very communicative, especially when it comes to himself. But I have seen enough of him and his action under circumstances which give me a great deal of pride. I have always felt that he was much finer in texture than his Dad, and still think so. It must be that he gets it from his mother.

Jim's relationship to Ola is harder to understand. As my father once told me, "Daddy was too hard on Mama." At the same time, he kept her on a pedestal, though that in itself may have been a way to avoid the kind of intimacy that characterized the marriage of Bob and Anne. But in that same "engagement letter" Jim's praise of Ola rings with genuine respect:

> And when it comes to that subject, as you know I am especially weak. She has always commanded the greatest love and affection I could give, but through the years her grip on me has grown stronger and stronger as my admiration for her many sterling points of character have become more and more outstanding. She has imparted to all of her children a courage, an ambition, and a practical sense of achievement; and along with it she has always stood for the fine, the beautiful, the pure, the lovely, the artistic. Under pressure, her courage does not know a single flinching nerve. I have seen her tried, and she has steadied me. Her combination would be hard to match. So I guess that is why I think as I do of her oldest living son, because I know that he has a great deal of her in him.

In this as in other letters Jim sounds like a man who has learned a hard lesson, but he continued to sleep alone in the upstairs bedroom.

The house was empty in those years, except for the two of them.

He comes in from the stable after dark, washes up, and eats a bite of supper—cold fried chicken from dinner, cold butter beans, which he prefers that way, a glass of buttermilk. If it is summer, the evening is already well advanced by the time he finishes his meal. He and Ola pass a silent hour in the sitting room, she doing handwork, he reading *Little Dorrit*. They are not angry with each other or nursing old grievances. It's just that she is growing so deaf that he can no longer make himself understood easily enough to carry on a conversation. When he tries to tell her something, she says, Don't shout, Mr. Kilgo.

She gets up. She thinks she'll go on to bed. He escorts her to the door, kisses her on the cheek, shouts, Sleep tight.

Then he turns out the lamps and, holding his place in the book with his index finger, climbs the wide staircase in the dimly lit back hall. He can hear her as he climbs, stirring about in the room off to the right.

It's hot upstairs, the dead air cooked all day beneath the tin roof. Because of banks of windows in the outside walls of the room where he sleeps, he calls that room the sleeping porch. The windows have been open all day, but still the room is permeated by the smell of stale tobacco smoke, and not a breath of air is stirring. Crickets and katydids make such a racket that they sound as though they are inside the room. He turns on the bedside lamp, plugs in an oscillating fan anchored heavily on the dresser, aimed at the bed, and undresses—tie, shirt and trousers, which he hangs neatly across the back of a chair.

In underwear and glasses he lies down on top of the sheet, lights a Chesterfield from the pack by the lamp, and opens *Little Dorrit*. The town clock, two blocks away, strikes the hour, eleven o'clock, but he counts the strokes anyway. He has read *Little Dorrit* before, but he never tires of Dickens. In that dark underside of London, he can easily lose himself.

Ola might have him back downstairs now, she's hinted that she might, but he won't ask. He's not ready yet to return to her bed. He doesn't deserve to.

He thinks of the woman, hears her name in his head, and notices his legs, how thin they are, and rubbed clean of hair.

IV

The child who stood at the window crying for his parents to come back and take him home to his grandfather is past fifty now, the house on St. John's Street has long since passed into other hands, and his father is dead. The man is holding a letter—a piece of a letter actually, the first page of the only surviving letter from his grandfather to him. It was written in the fall of 1944 while the boy's father was away in OCS and he and his little sister and their mother were staying at her parents' home in Greenwood. The page is stained and yellow and tearing along the folds. "My dear little Boy," it begins.

> I have been thinking about you all day, and as I promised to write to you, I came to the office after supper tonight so I could write you a letter with the typewriter. It is the same typewriter that you have written so much on, and I have drawn a picture of Pop at the machine. I don't think it is very good of Pop or the typewriter either, but it may help you visualize what I am doing. You can get your Mama to tell you what visualize means. I'm afraid the word imagination would be just as hard for you.

He goes on to say that without the little boy to remind him to check the mail on the way to church that morning he almost forgot to stop at the post office, and when he went through the vestibule, he paid no attention to the bell rope because the little boy who liked to stop and pull it was not there. The rest of the page is devoted to a sermon on good behavior and the importance of being unselfish. Then silence.

I look at the self-portrait he made, to help me "visualize" him, he said. It is drawn in pencil with a light, uncertain hand, pathetically childish. Yet it works, far more effectively than he could have dreamed, for I am looking at it from the Pearl Street sidewalk on a cold Sunday night through the gilt lettering of the showroom window: DARLINGTON MOTOR COMPANY. The door to his office is ajar. The drawn figure at the desk, washed in fluorescent light, begins to breathe. He is fifty-nine years old and feeling every year. That old weakness on his left side has been bothering him again, causing him to snap at Ola— to mistreat her, to be honest—and he is sorry he bullied that new stable boy earlier in the afternoon. He wants to be a better man than he is, he wants friends, he wants to be understood. He pecks at the keys: *My dear Bob.*

I am tempted to knock lightly at the door, confident that he will recognize me the second he sees my face. But there is another page to that letter. I don't know what became of it— it was always missing—but I bet it was all about horses, about how he had one picked out for me, a nice sorrel mare, and it would not be long before I would be old enough to care for her myself, and about how he had been looking forward for a long time to the day when we could ride together, side by side down Pine Haven Lane.

I take out a snapshot of him, Jim Kilgo, coming toward the camera on horseback. He is riding in from the left, coming on strong, necktie and hat, the big dark horse sleek with sweat, throwing its head, nostrils flared, plunging against the bit.